T0318626

# Cambridge Elements ☰

Elements in Earth System Governance
edited by
Frank Biermann
*Utrecht University*
Aarti Gupta
*Wageningen University*

# DELIBERATIVE GLOBAL GOVERNANCE

John S. Dryzek
*University of Canberra*

Quinlan Bowman
*University of Chicago*

Jonathan Kuyper
*Queen's University Belfast*

Jonathan Pickering
*University of Canberra*

Jensen Sass
*University of Canberra*

Hayley Stevenson
*Torcuato Di Tella University*

CAMBRIDGE
UNIVERSITY PRESS

# CAMBRIDGE
## UNIVERSITY PRESS

University Printing House, Cambridge CB2 8BS, United Kingdom

One Liberty Plaza, 20th Floor, New York, NY 10006, USA

477 Williamstown Road, Port Melbourne, VIC 3207, Australia

314–321, 3rd Floor, Plot 3, Splendor Forum, Jasola District Centre,
New Delhi – 110025, India

79 Anson Road, #06–04/06, Singapore 079906

Cambridge University Press is part of the University of Cambridge.

It furthers the University's mission by disseminating knowledge in the pursuit of
education, learning, and research at the highest international levels of excellence.

www.cambridge.org
Information on this title: www.cambridge.org/9781108732369
DOI: 10.1017/9781108762922

First published 2019

A catalogue record for this publication is available from the British Library.

ISBN 978-1-108-73236-9 Paperback
ISSN 2631-7818 (online)
ISSN 2631-780X (print)

# Deliberative Global Governance

## Elements in Earth System Governance

DOI: 10.1017/9781108762922
First published online: July 2019

John S. Dryzek
*University of Canberra*

Quinlan Bowman
*University of Chicago*

Jonathan Kuyper
*Queen's University Belfast*

Jonathan Pickering
*University of Canberra*

Jensen Sass
*University of Canberra*

Hayley Stevenson
*Torcuato Di Tella University*

**Abstract:** Global institutions are afflicted by severe democratic deficits, while many of the major problems facing the world remain intractable. Against this backdrop, we explore the prospects for a deliberative approach that puts effective, inclusive, and transformative communication at the heart of global governance. This approach can advance both democratic legitimacy and effective problem-solving. Existing institutions such as multilateral negotiations, international organizations, regimes, governance networks, and scientific assessments can be rendered more deliberative and democratic. Such reforms can pave the way for more thoroughgoing transformations in the global order that could involve citizens' assemblies, nested forums stretching from the local to the global, transnational citizens' juries and other mini-publics, crowdsourcing, and a global dissent channel. Equally important, though less easily designed, is the deliberative role of global civil society. We show how different institutional and civil society elements can be linked to good effect in a global deliberative system. The capacity of deliberative institutions to revise their own structures and processes means that deliberative global governance is not just a framework but also a reconstructive learning process. We pay special attention to climate change, peacebuilding, and global poverty.

**Keywords:** deliberative democracy, global governance, deliberative governance, international organizations, international regimes, global civil society, mini-publics

ISBNs: 9781108732369 (PB), 9781108762922 (OC)
ISSNs: 2631-7818 (online), 2631-780X (print)

# Contents

# 1 Introduction: In Search of Global Democracy

It is widely recognized that international bodies and organizations such as the United Nations, the World Trade Organization (WTO), the International Monetary Fund (IMF), and the G20 currently suffer severe democratic deficits (Nye 2001; Zürn 2018). They often fail to operate transparently and accountably, can be impervious to public criticism, and privilege some interests (e.g., in economic growth) over the broader range of values held by people across the world. Moreover, these undemocratic global institutions have often performed poorly in solving key transnational problems. For example, the last demonstrably effective multilateral global environmental agreement remains the 1987 Montreal Protocol for the protection of stratospheric ozone (some progress on climate change in the 2015 Paris Agreement notwithstanding). We intend to show that a deliberative approach to global governance can advance both democratic legitimacy and effective problem-solving.

## 1.1 Deliberative Democracy

Deliberative democracy reconceptualizes governance as effective, inclusive, and transformative communication encompassing citizens and policymakers. The basic idea, applicable globally no less than at other levels of governance, is that the legitimacy of any collective decision rests on the right, capacity, and opportunity of those subject to or affected by that decision (or their representatives) to participate in deliberation that is consequential for the content of the decision. Deliberation is noncoercive, reflective communication about matters of common concern, in which people try to communicate in terms that make sense to those with different starting points or frameworks. Thus, it entails giving reasons, respect for others, effective listening, and openness to change in positions if persuaded. Participants grant equal and adequate opportunities to one another (e.g., to offer reasons in support of and against various proposals) and they assume certain responsibilities (e.g., to listen actively and to make a sincere effort to understand others' perspectives).

Deliberative democracy is now well established in political theory, empirical social science, and institutional practice and experimentation, though the real world of governance generally falls far short of deliberative ideals. Deliberative democrats have their eyes on whole systems of governance – not just isolated institutional experiments. Unlike more familiar conceptions of democracy, deliberative democracy can apply to contexts where elections are unavailable – such as global governance – though if elections are available, deliberation can fruitfully coexist with them.

We will argue that deliberative global governance can empower the global community to make more legitimate and effective decisions to the benefit of present and future generations. A deliberative approach offers a way out of current impasses in global governance and a vision for its future. This approach can draw on the wisdom of communities directly affected by climate change, violent conflict, extreme poverty, and other global problems to develop solutions that will best serve humanity's needs and interests. We base our claims and proposals not just on reasoning about what is possible but also on evidence from existing deliberative practice. We are well aware of relevant limitations on the respective capacities of citizens, political leaders, and political systems but at the same time believe that capacities can be developed. We draw on our own research and scholarship and that of others, integrating and extending them into a statement of what deliberative global governance can and should entail.

## 1.2 Why Deliberative Democracy Applies to the Global Level

Some existing proposals for global democracy, especially those involving an elected UN Parliamentary Assembly (Falk and Strauss 2011), think of democratic aspirations in terms of a people (or demos) with a shared political identity coupled with a robust set of authoritative institutions of the sort found in liberal democratic states. Critics of global democracy dismiss such proposals as utopian and out of step with the realities of international relations (for example, Keohane 2015).

But global democratization does not have to follow the democratic institutions found in nation-states (Kuyper and Dryzek 2016). Moreover, proposals for global democracy modeled on national templates often misread history. In many countries, a shared national identity emerged only *after* state institutions took shape, and key democratic mechanisms such as curbs on arbitrary state power often came well before elections (Goodin 2010). Any realizable vision for global democratization needs to take as its starting point important circumstances and constraints that are likely to operate for the foreseeable future, including the absence of a centralized world government and far greater cultural and institutional heterogeneity than exists within any one state.

A deliberative approach enables creativity in thinking about how to reduce the global democratic deficit in feasible ways, which do not require a unitary global demos or a global state, let alone global elections. Instead of a global demos, it is possible to think in terms of diverse global publics, already found around areas of common concern, from climate change to international trade to human rights. In the absence of recourse to centralized means of exercising legitimate coercive force, other ways of coordinating global action prove crucial, including persuasion and deliberation. Rather than resting hopes on a global parliament or the like, legitimate representation can be conceptualized in broader terms, such as ensuring that the range of discourses to which people subscribe – including those embodying values such as concern for the vulnerable and respect for nature – is reflected in global decision-making bodies.

Any reconfiguration of global governance ought to be acceptable to different peoples around the world. This is especially true for a specifically democratic mode, which must respect the autonomy and equality of different people and peoples, and cannot be foisted upon them. Deliberation meets this standard because, although manifested differently across time and space, it is a cultural universal. All societies feature a disposition for people to exchange reasons and arguments, listen to one another, and take decisions on that basis. Amartya Sen (2003) points out that while democracy as voting is a Western ideal, democracy as public reasoning, or deliberation, can be found in all societies. Different cultures will embody and formalize deliberation in a variety of ways: Some may promote consensual agreement while others will honor contestation; some will require particular rituals as necessary; norms vary concerning who can say what. Sass and Dryzek (2014: 3) describe how, in myriad cultures, deliberation occurs such that "publicly accessible meanings, symbols, and norms shape the way political actors engage one another in discourse."

All the world's major religions endorse an ethic of reciprocity – treat others as you would like them to treat you (Neusner and Chilton 2009) – as do many moral codes. Experiments in many countries confirm that people will seek such reciprocity even at personal material cost (Henrich et al. 2004: 8). Translating this into *deliberative* reciprocity, which requires an effort to both reach and understand differently situated others, is often challenging, and in practice conflicts, hierarchies, and oppressive discourses intervene. Still, reciprocity norms are available as resources for promoting mutual justification in many religious, moral, and cultural traditions.

Because deliberation occurs even in states where the reach of constitutions is weak, it suits the global arena, which lacks an overarching constitutional framework. Deliberative global governance recognizes the vast range of communicative possibilities from different cultural contexts and seeks to incorporate those forms in transnational dialogue.

## 1.3 Preview

We intend to show that global democracy requires a meaningful and inclusive deliberative system that effectively links publics, discourses, representatives, and institutions.

We begin by elucidating the basic justification for deliberative global governance. At its heart, as we asserted at the outset, deliberative democracy offers an account of legitimate governance – we show how deliberative legitimacy can be applied globally. Deliberation also enables accountability in settings where the familiar mechanism of accountability via electoral judgment on the performance of leaders is unavailable. We argue further that public deliberation can generate effective solutions for collective problems. After elaborating how deliberative legitimacy, accountability, and effectiveness can work in practice in global politics, we demonstrate that deliberative democracy can make sense of – and if necessary confront – different sorts of power.

The deliberative approach can be applied to reform of existing global institutions and practices as well as the design of new ones. For existing institutions, we show how more inclusive and authentic deliberation can be sought in multilateral negotiations, international organizations and regimes, global constitutionalism and its pluralistic alternative, transnational governance networks, and scientific assessments. These kinds of improvements can pave the way for more thoroughgoing deliberative and democratic reconfiguration. For this larger change, we set out principles for a Deliberative Global Citizens' Assembly (DGCA), which could function in different ways, including as a second chamber for the UN General Assembly), nested deliberative forums in layers from the local to the global, transnational citizens' juries and related "mini-publics," deliberative crowdsourcing, and a global dissent channel. We demonstrate how such innovations are both financially affordable and feasible. Aside from formal institutions, deliberative governance needs healthy transnational public spheres and effective representation from global civil society, based in turn on effective engagement across different discourses (including reformist and radical discourses).

We show how these various practices and innovations can be integrated in global deliberative systems that join top-down and bottom-up governance (making sense of what is sometimes called "hybrid multilateralism"). Deliberative systems encompass stakeholders, civil society, expert communities, state representatives and policymakers, linking decision-making bodies with larger processes in the public sphere. It is each system as a whole that should yield authentic, inclusive, and effective deliberation – not just its components. The deliberative system idea can redeem the promise of "polycentric" governance and ensure that the variety of polycentric initiatives adds up to an effective response to a shared problem.

Institutional design can and should itself be deliberative and participatory, so deliberative global governance is both a framework and a process of reconstructive learning. Once established, deliberative institutions should reveal a reflexive capacity to revise their structures and processes upon reflection on their own performance, avoiding the inability to reform themselves that many international organizations currently suffer.

We explain how deliberative global governance can respond effectively to key global problems, notably climate change, armed conflict, and poverty. We indicate how a deliberative systems conceptualization of global climate governance offers a framework for more effective and ambitious action. We point to the strong affinities between deliberative governance and effective peacebuilding both within and across national boundaries. Finally, we describe how global poverty can be confronted through a deliberative approach to global justice involving direct participation by the poor – not just those (such as NGOs) who claim to speak on their behalf.

## 2 Why Deliberative Global Governance?

There are three key reasons to prioritize deliberative global governance: the legitimacy it can afford to collective decisions, the accountability it can enable, and its potential effectiveness in solving pressing problems. These reasons prove mutually reinforcing. We now show how legitimacy, accountability, and effectiveness can be achieved in practice, and how to confront and cope with questions of power that stand in the way of deliberative governance.

## 2.1 Legitimacy

Legitimacy means that those who make rules or decisions do so in justified ways. Scholars commonly differentiate "normative" and "sociological" legitimacy. Normative legitimacy entails theorists and practitioners determining *ex ante* good standards with which rule-makers must comply. Standards might involve due process, respect for rights, or consent of the governed. For deliberative democracy, the standards include: due process (searching out policies that are acceptable to all affected or subjected); rights of free expression and to justification from authority-holders (see our discussion of accountability in Section 2.2); and consent to authority through public deliberation. It is through deliberation that people can have their say about policies affecting their welfare.

In sociological terms, government is legitimate insofar as those subjected to and affected by public decisions *believe* it is rightful. However, from a deliberative perspective, it is not enough for the "global governors" who make and implement rules (Avant, Finnemore, and Sell 2010: 1–31) to take account of public opinion. Public opinion can rest on misunderstandings and unreflective assumptions. Deliberation puts these ideas to the test insofar as participants explain and justify relevant beliefs, preferences, and positions to each other. It is the result of this engagement that ought to be reflected in legitimate collective decisions. In an experimental design, Esaiasson, Gilljam, and Persson (2017) find that affected individuals are more likely to accept decisions when decision-makers clearly listen and explain, rather than just follow majority opinion. Birnbaum, Bodin, and Sandström (2015) find that in a natural resource management case, the deliberative qualities of the process mattered more for perceived legitimacy than more general democratic qualities.

On the face of it, advances in communications technology mean that exposure to different perspectives is stronger now than ever (though nearly half of the world's population still lacks Internet access; Internet World Stats 2018). However, all is not well in deliberative terms, as people often encase themselves in social media "echo chambers" where they share ideas only with like-minded others and avoid challenge from different viewpoints. Exposure to different ideas can be sought online (Coleman and Moss 2012), but more organized face-to-face settings (of the sort we outline in Section 4) provide opportunities for encountering diverse others in more deliberative fashion.

Sociological legitimacy (as well as normative legitimacy) does of course require that the results of such deliberative engagements somehow be transmitted to empowered institutions or processes. Along these lines, the United Nations has experimented with a range of participatory approaches such as the surveys, electronic forums, workshops, civil society dialogues, and crowdsourcing (of highly variable deliberative quality) that fed into the adoption of the Sustainable Development Goals (SDGs) in 2015 (see Section 4.4).

For deliberative democrats, normative legitimacy does not mean that all ideas generated in public dialogue are equally worthy of consideration. Public deliberation can sort good arguments and considerations from bad ones. However, it is not appropriate to adopt a simple measure of "true" and "false" when determining which ideas are worthy. On most important issues there will be competing knowledge claims. The challenge for deliberative democracy is to maintain genuine respect for diversity without succumbing to an unhelpful relativism.

In practice, public deliberation will implicate elements of judgment, as well as objective truth and falsity. For instance, the World Health Organization (WHO) and Joint United Nations Programme on HIV/AIDS (UNAID's) joint consultations on circumcision as a preventative health measure had to contend with claims about the relationship between circumcision and religious/cultural purity, risk and proportionality, children's rights, etc. The verifiable fact that circumcised heterosexual males are 60 percent less likely to contract HIV could not be the sole basis for deciding to adopt this as a WHO recommendation. The decision also needed to take into account social values and cultural practices (Peltzer et al. 2007; WHO 2007).

Engagement across different discourses, and the ensuing transmission of the outcome into decision-making processes, should ideally be achieved in a deliberative fashion. Such engagement allows for the possibility of developing mutual understanding, and perhaps even shared perspectives, and ultimately strengthens the capacity to be self-critical. A norm of inclusion has produced widespread civil society participation in international institutions (see Section 3.2). But these practices often fall far short of deliberative ideals. Shortcomings include an emphasis on the opportunity to speak without any assurance of being listened to or understood; dominance of participants from the Global North; and a tendency toward participatory performance with little impact on actual decisions. These deficiencies detract from the legitimacy of global governance but can be overcome.

## 2.2 Accountability

Accountability is a key ingredient of legitimacy. Within states, accountability is normally thought of in terms of governments being held accountable at periodic elections. However, accountability can be construed more broadly as involving rule-makers explaining their decisions and actions to rule-takers (those subject to collective decisions), with the latter being able to sanction the former if those explanations are found wanting (Grant and Keohane 2005). Accountability, then, intrinsically contains a deliberative element, insofar as decisions must be explained and justified to others, with the quality and type of explanation being important when it comes to how rule-takers opt to sanction the rule-makers (for example, by voting them out of office). At the global level, deliberation is even more crucial for accountability. Because electoral mechanisms do not exist, accountability must focus on giving an account – to other organizations and governments, to civil society, and to citizens – and on responding to questioning.

Those who make and implement rules and decisions ought to be accountable to those affected by or subjected to those rules and decisions. These global governors can be found in intergovernmental institutions (like the World Bank or the United Nations), as well as in private institutions that exercise authority (like the Forest Stewardship Council or The Global Fund to Fight AIDS, Tuberculosis and Malaria). They include leaders of organizations, states, funding agencies, courts, and investors.

International Relations scholars typically think of accountability in principal–agent terms: states (principals) delegate authority to international institutions (agents), and these institutions must be accountable to their member states. From this perspective, the World Bank would be accountable if its President and Executive Directors explained to the member countries represented on its Board of Governors how the Bank's policies and activities reflect these members' preferences (in annual reports and meetings). Any deviation from member-state preferences could then be exposed or punished by withholding funds or refusing to renew contracts.

Deliberative global governance entails a more expansive notion of accountability, especially in terms of the accountability "audience" (*to whom* governors ought to be accountable) and how accountability is achieved. Limiting the accountability audience to nation-states is insufficient. Many states are themselves undemocratic, leaving their citizens without any chain of accountability linking them democratically to international institutions. Even for citizens of democratic states, accountability is diluted when it is filtered through state representatives.

People affected by the decisions of international institutions will not usually have the capacity to sanction these institutions for abuses of power or poor choices. However, accountability does not always have to be punitive to be effective. A more expansive notion of accountability sees it as a mechanism for social learning. The requirement to explain and justify one's decisions and actions to a wider audience can prompt consideration of the needs, interests, and perspectives of audience members. When power-holders are obliged to try to explain their actions in terms that the audience will understand and accept, there is a possibility for reflection, learning, and attention to the consequences of their actions (Benhabib 1996: 71–72). These virtuous effects can be enhanced by a deliberative form of accountability.

Deliberative accountability involving anything like the full participation of an audience is rarely, if ever, practiced in international politics. More common is "narrative accountability" in Mansbridge's (2009: 384) terms, whereby institutions provide an account of their actions and decisions. Even the UN Security Council (UNSC), one of the most closed institutions in the international system, has introduced monthly "dialogues" between its president and civil society organizations to "advance transparency and accountability within the UN system" (WFUNA 2018). These meetings would be more appropriately called "briefings" because the style of exchange lacks a two-way questioning and answering that would characterize dialogue and deliberation. Two-way exchanges can already be found in the peer review practices of international organizations, for example when the Organization for Economic Cooperation and Development (OECD's) Development Assistance Committee reviews a country's practices in providing assistance to poorer countries – though these are not very democratic, given that accountability is considered due only to the international organization and its member governments. International institutions do often recognize that accountability is important, including accountability to actors beyond nation-states. Transforming their limited accountability practices into deliberative accountability would advance the democratization of global governance, to the degree such practices become consequential for collective decisions.

## 2.3 Effectiveness: Compliance and the Common Good

Deliberative governance is valuable not just for intrinsic democratic reasons of legitimacy and accountability but also for the instrumental reason that it can enable progress in addressing collective problems – including complex and seemingly intractable ones, such as climate change, violent conflict, and extreme poverty, which we will address later. Intrinsic and instrumental reasons are linked here because democratic legitimacy can help secure compliance with collective decisions (see Section 2.3). Inclusive deliberation facilitates effective implementation of decisions inasmuch as it generates outcomes broadly recognized as legitimate. This does not mean implementation is automatic, only that decisions produced by inclusive public deliberation should generally provoke less resistance and be more likely to be implemented than decisions produced by power-politics and strategizing.

Addressing many global problems (such as climate change) relies upon overcoming free-riding, where individual countries or other actors seek to avoid contributing to the collective effort, while benefitting from the contributions of others. This means that commitment to collective decisions can be hard to secure. Deliberative processes promote common interests and public goods; arguments couched in such terms are more persuasive than those couched in terms of private interests. There is plenty of evidence here from experiments and small-scale forums on climate change, genetic technologies, and other issues (Stevenson and Dryzek 2014: 20–21). The success of norm entrepreneurs – those who seek to convince governments, organizations, societies, and corporations to adopt new standards to guide actions – in international politics depends crucially on their ability to convince others that the norm in question (be it a human right or a rule of war or environmental conservation) is a fundamental common interest (Finnemore and Sikkink 1998). And parties to international negotiations often strive to couch their positions in terms of public goods, which helps explain the pervasiveness of implicit and explicit claims about justice in climate change negotiations. The efforts of norm entrepreneurs and justice advocates can meet with resistance, not least from those subscribing to different norms or definitions of justice. But when this happens, deliberation should typically be able to reconcile differences about what the common good entails.

## 2.4 Effectiveness: Slow Thinking and Creative Outcomes

Deliberation can further generate effective solutions because it embodies "slow thinking" in Kahneman's (2011) terms. Work in cognitive psychology has shown that humans are "hard-wired" to be overconfident in their decision-making skills, while making systematic errors in their reasoning. This, Kahneman explains, is because human decision-making typically deploys only one of two available cognitive systems: System 1, which is fast, intuitive, and effortless, rather than System 2, which is slow, calculated, and effortful.

System 1 can lead people to misunderstand their own preferences, neglect the future, and underestimate risks. System 2, in contrast, helps people align their preferences with their values, take due consideration of how decisions relate to the future, and unpack the risks involved in these choices. As Kahneman and others have noted, System 2 is the realm of *deliberation* (in the personal as well as the social sense): slow and reasoned thinking about choices and their implications. While it is cognitively demanding to engage System 2, it leads to much better decision-making. Inculcating deliberation in governance systems is therefore a crucial way to make decisions that are more effective (i.e., not based on flawed reasoning). A paradigm example of slow thinking would be the deliberations of the Executive Committee convened to advise President John F. Kennedy on a response to the Soviet Union's deployment of nuclear missiles in Cuba (Allison 1971), which managed to avoid nuclear war. A paradigm example of fast thinking can be found in President Donald Trump's tweets, riddled with factual inaccuracy, snap reactions, and prejudice. Comprehending and tackling climate change requires moving from fast System 1 thinking to the slower ruminations of System 2. Because climate change is a complex, multifaceted issue, deliberation in System 2 can allow individuals to understand probabilities of different climate-induced problems (such as the pros and cons of different climate models), see how these problems affect others on the ground, and comprehend the long-term (temporal) nature of the issue (Kahneman 2018).

In recognizing the benefits of deliberation for avoiding System 1 biases, decision-makers can take their time over decisions, ensuring that new frameworks, situated knowledge, and information feed into policy formation and implementation. The need for time does not excuse inaction: As the Cuban missile case shows, slow thinking can be deployed in short order to respond to a crisis.

## 2.5 Effectiveness: The Epistemic Argument

Democracy in general can promote effective collective problem-solving as it mobilizes "the wisdom of crowds." As Landemore (2013) points out, democracy – rule of the many – generally leads to smarter decisions than either rule of the few (technocracy or oligarchy) or rule of the one (autocracy). This is because democracy harnesses cognitive diversity, which overcomes the inevitable limits to the information processing and reasoning capacities of individuals. But, as Landemore points out, the wisdom of crowds requires more than just an aggregation of different views: Rather, people need to be in effective deliberative interaction with each other to better share and integrate knowledge.

Deliberation is well suited to tackle complex problems because it can interpret and integrate views and bits of knowledge from different directions (disciplines, frameworks, interests, values, or concerns) relevant to different facets of complex problems. Such knowledge is often dispersed across differently situated individuals, groups, and organizations – possibly at different levels from the local to the global. Deliberation enables such actors to air views, perceive and create interconnections, and identify knowledge gaps necessary to tackle emergent problems. Deliberation is valuable here as it can induce people concerned with different aspects of problems to find meaningful ways to communicate and cooperate with each other.

The knowledge required to respond effectively to global challenges is widely dispersed. Pervasive ignorance and the deprivation of basic needs inhibit participation and limit the ability to harness cognitive diversity. Global democratization requires ameliorating these problems (Stevenson 2016), but their persistence does not negate the instrumental value of drawing diverse perspectives into deliberation and decision-making.

Two examples illustrate the dangers of epistemic exclusion in global governance. In 2011, the Independent Evaluation Office of the IMF conducted an inquiry into why the institution failed to anticipate the 2008 global financial crisis. Their findings pointed to "groupthink" and a "lack of incentives to . . . raise contrarian views." They observed a prevailing view among staff that "market discipline and self-regulation would be sufficient to stave off serious problems" (IEO 2011: 1–7). Evans and Finnemore (2001: 9–12) describe the epistemic homogeneity in the IMF as the result of "intellectual monocropping." Their analysis of IMF recruitment strategies found a strong emphasis on elite institutional education and competence in a dominant macroeconomic paradigm. The result was an overwhelmingly high proportion of male staff with doctoral degrees from North American universities. No staff members were trained outside an industrialized country. Diversifying the staff profiles of international institutions is one way to minimize epistemic limitations, but tapping into the insights of people affected by international institutions is also important.

The international community's response to natural disasters further illustrates the impact of epistemic limitations. Female mortality figures are often considerably higher than male mortality figures when natural disasters strike (Neumayer and Plümper 2007). In the 2004 Indian Ocean Tsunami, four times as many women died as men (MacDonald 2005). The factors underpinning female mortality here are often beyond the lived experience of policymakers. In the case of the Tsunami, the discrepancy is explained by social, cultural, and biological factors. Norms and dress codes mean males learn to run, climb, and swim more than females; and women are typically less physically strong than men, especially during pregnancy. Women may be less likely to seek safety if they remain in their homes caring for children, the elderly, and sick. Humanitarian agencies focus narrowly on food and water in the aftermath of disasters. Menstrual hygiene has long been a blind spot. To avoid asking men for clean cloths, women and girls have often resorted to washing menstrual cloths in contaminated water, exposing them to infections (WHO 2002). Without efforts to tap into the knowledge and insights of different people, problems like these often go unnoticed by decision-makers.

In sum, reasoned and inclusive deliberation can foster effective governance by promoting acceptance of and so compliance with collective decisions, shifting individuals into slow thinking and so smarter decisions. Global governance can thrive on diversity – engaging people from different nations, organizations, races, ethnicities, social classes, genders, and religions – but only to the degree disparate views are harnessed effectively in deliberative terms.

## 2.6 Confronting Power

Before moving to how deliberative global governance can be pursued in and through institutions, we respond to a standard criticism: that deliberative democrats are insufficiently attentive to questions of power. Indeed, one can point to deliberative practices that can be subverted by unjust or coercive power relations. But so it is with any conception of democracy and its associated practices. A more interesting question is: Does foregrounding deliberation lead to greater or less attention to power than otherwise might be the case?

An emphasis on deliberation highlights power relations, rather than concealing or ignoring them. Among deliberative democrats, there is widespread agreement that *coercive* power should ideally be absent from deliberative procedures and practices (Mansbridge et al. 2010: 72). Noncoercive power can be found in the ability of deliberation itself to lead participants to resist coercion – if, for example, they come to realize that collectively they can effectively refuse to be intimidated by a repressive government (Curato, Hammond, and Min 2019).

However, it is doubtful that most real-world deliberations could ever be fully "coercion-free" – either because coercion creeps into the forum itself (for example, if a representative of a small poor state fears the financial consequences of opposing the position of a large donor state) or because coercion subverts the process from outside (for example, if participants set aside a justifiable proposal, dreading the reaction it might provoke from populist demagogues or irresponsible journalists). Dominant discourses such as neoliberalism in global financial affairs can distort communication and repress alternatives. However, as we will illustrate later, deliberative practices and processes offer many ways of expanding the range of perspectives and considerations that are brought to bear on global decision-making. In this way, they could counteract dominant discourses that serve some interests and repress others, increasing the likelihood that global decision-making will take account of interests and perspectives that would otherwise be ignored or suppressed.

Here it is important to analyze power relations that may subvert deliberative *and* non-deliberative decision-making practices. Deliberation has often been defined in opposition to voting (Mansbridge et al. 2010: 64). Yet deliberative democrats recognize that deliberation can set the stage for other forms of decision-making, such as voting and negotiation; it is not necessarily a wholesale alternative to them. Coercion can subvert non-deliberative democratic practices as well as deliberative ones (consider voter intimidation). And the ability of deliberation itself to generate resistance to coercion may help free such non-deliberative practices from the grip of coercion – if, for example, voters realize that collectively they can resist intimidation, or small poor states develop solidarity against a wealthy large state in the context of international negotiations.

As an ideal for decision-making, deliberation leads us to criticize conditions that undermine participants' abilities to reflect on their preferences, values, and interests in a noncoercive fashion. Some constraints are easily justifiable (consider time limits). Others bear a much higher burden of justification (consider decisions to exclude would-be participants on the grounds they would undermine the deliberative qualities of a process; this could apply, for example, to climate change deniers mobilized and financed by fossil fuel corporations). In any case, treating deliberation as an aspirational ideal (Mansbridge et al. 2010: 65) provides us with a benchmark for criticizing power relations, be they subtle hierarchies within a process or strategic attempts to manipulate a process from the outside.

Take the deliberative criterion that participants should have equal and adequate opportunities to set the agenda. From this perspective, dominant discourses such as neoliberalism in global financial affairs can be criticized if they distort communication or repress alternatives. Or consider the criterion that participants should have equal and adequate opportunities to offer reasons in support of and against various proposals. From this perspective, an exclusive reliance on certain speech styles (such as dispassionate argument) can be criticized insofar as they serve the interests of the articulate and powerful, marginalizing others. Or consider the criterion that participants should seek out mutually acceptable and generally accessible reasons for their policy preferences (Gutmann and Thompson 2004). From this perspective, rhetoric that mobilizes irrationality and sectarian division (such as Donald Trump's aggressive nationalism) is undesirable, and rhetoric that bridges across deep difference (for example, Mikhail Gorbachev's invocation of a "common European home" in helping to defuse the Cold War in Europe) is praiseworthy.

Likewise, deliberative criteria point to practical recommendations to counter certain power relations. If, in principle, all affected parties are to be included on equal terms, that means there may be a need for historically disadvantaged groups to develop deliberative capacities in protected spaces (enclaves) before engaging with the rest of the deliberative system: for example, in the International Indigenous Forum on Biodiversity that accompanies meetings of the UN Convention on Biological Diversity.

Having set out the basic reasons for prioritizing deliberative global governance and having shown how mechanisms might operate to support those reasons, we now explore how existing institutions can be made more deliberative, before examining the prospects for more thoroughgoing institutional transformation.

## 3 Making Existing Institutions and Practices More Deliberative

We will now provide good reasons to think that the global governance landscape can afford opportunities for deliberative democratization – though it will often be an uphill struggle. We explore the features of existing institutions that provide such opportunities, with a view to identifying pathways enabling more meaningful, inclusive, and consequential deliberation in the future.

### 3.1 Multilateral Negotiations

The strategic or rationalist theory of multilateral negotiations assumes that states seek to maximize their own interests. When they enter negotiations, it is to serve these interests rather than striving for cooperation or common good outcomes. But a growing number of studies have demonstrated the importance of argumentation in negotiations, and the prevalence of deliberation rather than just bargaining. These studies deploy constructivist or sociological institutionalist theory and therefore begin with different assumptions than rational choice theorists about the international system and its actors. From this perspective, scholars see states following a "logic of appropriateness" or "logic of argumentation" in an environment of institutionalized norms and knowledge (Risse 2000; Schimmelfennig 2001). These assumptions prompt scholars to look for evidence of reaching agreement through the mutual evaluation of arguments and "reasoned consensus" (Risse 2000: 9) rather than (only) through threats, promises, and the trading of favors. In this section we point to evidence of existing and potential argumentation in the practices and culture of multilateral negotiation, and identify necessary conditions for more deliberative negotiations.

There are some islands of deliberative practice in international negotiations, especially in the European Union (EU). Studies of EU negotiations reveal the positive role that normative argumentation can play in reaching agreement. In EU negotiations to expand membership to Central and Eastern Europe, Schimmelfennig found evidence of "rhetorical action," or the "strategic use of norm-based arguments" (2001). Opponents of expansion were "shamed" into accepting the norm-based arguments of expansion proponents because those arguments reflected the EU's norms and values. They could not reject the arguments without also rejecting the principles underpinning their own community.

In a study of EU negotiations on the Maritime Labour Convention (adopted in 2006 under the International Labour Organization), Riddervold found that negotiators at times used threats and self-interested arguments, but at other times used mutually acceptable argumentation to justify their positions. Moreover, it was deliberation and not bargaining that was more effective in producing agreement (Riddervold 2011: 576). Reinhard, Biesenbender, and Holzinger (2014: 283) analyzed EU negotiations on the Treaty of Amsterdam (which was adopted to amend the 1992 Treaty on European Union) and came to a similar conclusion, that "negotiators who use . . . normative arguments to back up a bargaining stance are able to impact the negotiation outcome to a greater extent than those who do not." Deliberation can therefore be effective for producing both agreement and more legitimate negotiation outcomes.

Deliberative principles are also at work in global climate change negotiations in the "indabas" inspired by a Zulu deliberative tradition. Indabas involved small facilitated groups of key negotiators, oriented toward open exchange of views and establishing common interests (Rathi 2015), helping negotiations move beyond impasse. There are ways to expand this deliberative logic. Indaba-like groups could strive to include members from different coalitions of countries (as the Open Working Group on the Sustainable Development Goals did; Chasek et al 2016). Some negotiations could take place under the auspices of a facilitator rather than a chair (though the constructive roles chairs can play should be recognized). The role of a facilitator in any process is to induce deliberative principles of respect, recognition, communicating in ways that make sense to those who do not share one's own worldview, effective listening, constructive proposal-making that meets core interests of different sides, and non-coercion. Ideally, participants themselves would devise these rules; experience suggests when they do so at the outset, they generally come up with very deliberative principles (reinforcing our claim that deliberation is a universal human capacity).

Deliberative negotiations require negotiators who are authorized to deliberate. Deliberative capacity in this setting is not evenly distributed: Some actors have greater capacity than others by virtue of the authority bestowed on them by their governments. Negotiators are state representatives; to represent their states effectively in negotiations they need to be permitted a degree of independent judgment. Without such discretion, or "slack," they cannot react to changing situations, and negotiations become hamstrung (Odell 2000: 159). But state representatives in any multilateral negotiation will vary in their degree of authority and discretion. Some governments keep their representatives on a tighter leash than others. Moving toward deliberative modes of negotiation requires negotiators to have the discretion to reflect on and evaluate the reasons and arguments they hear, and to adjust their negotiation position accordingly.

Just as important as formal institutional practices are the culture and norms pervading multilateral negotiations. Hopmann (1995: 24) suggests that many negotiators have been socialized into a realist paradigm of negotiation, in which distributive bargaining over fixed payoffs is all that occurs. Diplomats put into practice their taught theory, and university training does not usually involve deliberative negotiation. The university is therefore an important site for fostering a new culture and norms to enhance deliberation in global governance, as our earlier discussion of the hiring practices of the IMF suggests.

An alternative to the realist paradigm of distributive bargaining (focusing on the payoffs to each party secured at the expense of the others) is integrative bargaining. The focus of this problem-solving mode of negotiation is on identifying common or complementary interests and solutions among negotiating parties. This brings us closer to a deliberative mode of negotiation. Integrative bargaining is not just a theoretical possibility; many international environmental regimes have been formed in such a way (Young 1994: 117–139). This highlights the possibility of replacing the dominant realist culture of negotiation with something that incorporates principles of deliberative democracy.

Principles of justice are also finding a place in the culture of multilateral negotiations, especially over issues that feature strong differences of perspective between countries in the Global North and South, such as environmental problems. Negotiators often justify positions in the language of justice rather than self-interest. But from a deliberative perspective, this can still be deficient if justice is invoked in ways that merely serve self-interest. For example, in climate change negotiations, states such as China and India have used the historical justice argument to demand stronger commitments to reducing greenhouse gas emissions in developed countries and simultaneously to downplay their own obligation to reduce emissions. But these countries should also recognize – for the sake of credible argument – that the historical point also applies to their own subpopulations of relatively wealthy consumers, who have built prosperity on a history of fossil fuel use (Harris 2011: 647). Here it falls to other states to call for normative consistency and "entrap" China and India in their own arguments (Schimmelfennig 2001). Accepting consistency would mean increased obligations to reduce emissions on their part. It would also motivate other countries (notably industrialized societies) to be more credible and less self-serving in the justice arguments they make, improving deliberative quality all round.

## 3.2 International Organizations

For some scholars of international relations, the idea that international organizations (IOs) could be deliberative institutions would be incoherent. Realists understand IOs as mere instruments or resources of the most powerful state or states in the international system (such as the United States). But the aim to make IOs more deliberative begins to appear more feasible once we look beyond the realist paradigm to see how liberal and constructivist theory understands these institutions. For liberals, IOs are forums where states (and, increasingly, non-state actors) seek to deepen their interdependence in ways that are mutually useful for handling shared problems and opportunities. Constructivists also see IOs as forums, but their focus is on how shared norms and identities develop and diffuse in these environments.

There are some features of IOs as forums that are fortuitous for deliberation. While decision-making procedures vary among IOs, consensus is often prized as the ideal. Even among those IOs with voting procedures, a culture has developed that eschews voting and seeks decisions by consensus whenever possible. In the UN General Assembly, states make considerable effort to attract consensus for their proposed resolutions. This is one reason why the same resolutions are often introduced year after year: If a resolution has been adopted by majority vote, a state will often reintroduce it with a view to securing consensus (Panke 2014: 445–446). General Assembly resolutions are considered a reflection of global opinion; hence they carry more weight if adopted by consensus. This discourages states from articulating their preferences in purely self-interested ways; to achieve consensus they have to consider interests that are generalizable to all states, and common principles. Other states can see through insincerity and often refuse to support such resolutions (for example, India's proposed resolution on a Convention on the Prohibition on the Use of Nuclear Weapons; see Panke 2014: 448–450).

Consensus has its limitations, notably if it means simply seeking some lowest common denominator, which falls short of effectively addressing the problem at hand. Multilateral climate change negotiations have often been like this. Our claim is just that the consensus norm means there is likely to be more deliberation than there would be under competing principles such as simple majority rule.

The UNSC is the institution where great powers exert perhaps the strongest control in the international system, but here, too, consensus plays some role. To be adopted in the UNSC, a resolution requires the consensus of the five permanent members (China, Russia, US, France, and UK – the "P5"), as well as the support of four of the ten non-permanent members. Consensus has not always been dominant, but from 2001 to 2015 90 percent of all resolutions were adopted by consensus (von Einsiedel, Malone, and Ugarte 2015: 3). Given the contested legitimacy of permanent membership, the P5 have a strong interest in seeking resolutions by consensus because it improves the perceived legitimacy of decisions that automatically apply to all states in the international system. Of course, the closed nature of the forum makes it hard to know how consensus is achieved, and there is evidence to suggest that financial incentives play a part (e.g., Kuziemko and Werker 2006). But given that the members elected by the General Assembly (the "E10") often seek seats for reputational gain, one way to promote deliberation in the UNSC is to persuade these states to practice a deliberative style of participation.

Higgott and Erman (2010) find deliberative practices an effective way to address the legitimacy deficits of global economic institutions, particularly the WTO. They describe how the WTO can gain legitimacy to the degree it adopts deliberative practices of argumentation rather than bargaining, alongside more effective inclusion that overcomes existing power asymmetries across developed and developing countries. Milewicz and Goodin (2018) show that the Universal Periodic Review process carried out by the UN Human Rights Council has strong deliberative features that can even draw in countries with poor human rights performance, who need to secure respect from peer countries.

*Democratizing* the deliberative features of IOs is another challenge altogether. Here there are some causes for optimism because a norm of inclusion has diffused across IOs in recent years. This norm applies to states and non-state actors alike. Legitimacy challenges have forced small state-based "clubs" to open up to more member states. This trend is illustrated by the expanded participation in "Green Room" meetings of the WTO where the great powers used to meet in secret to hammer out deals before presenting them as faits accomplis to the rest of the international community (Singh 2015: 204). Another key example is the shift from the G7/8 to the G20 as the most important club for global economic governance, a shift provoked by the global economic crisis of 2008, which left emerging economies relatively unscathed and hence in a stronger position to assert their right to be included.

IOs are also increasingly open to stakeholder participation (Tallberg et al 2013). Scholte (2016: 717) argues that since the 1990s civil society consultations have become "a general norm of contemporary global governance." In Steffek and Nanz's (2008: 19–21) analysis of thirty-two European and global institutions, almost all provide arrangements for civil society consultation. This norm of inclusion is part of a wider pattern of IOs engaging with democratic principles. Dingwerth et al (2015) found a fourfold increase in IOs' use of democratic rhetoric (transparency, accountability, inclusiveness, representation, and participation) between 1980 and 2011. The challenge is to pressure these organizations to match their rhetoric with their actions, and this responsibility largely falls to global civil society. The democratic performance of IOs still falls far short of their rhetoric. Inclusion of non-state actors is often tokenistic. Civil society is generally consulted at the policy formation stage, excluded from decision-making, and included again in policy implementation (Tallberg et al 2013: 217). Attitudes such as "arrogance, inflexibility, reluctance, and secrecy" can also undermine the quality of consultations, as can poor preparation on the part of civil society, and dominance by elites and the Global North (Scholte 2016: 717). Mega-consultations – such as those undertaken during the planning of the SDGs – are generally under-representative of those in developing countries and struggle to affect collective decisions (Sénit et al. 2017).

International organizations could adopt minimum standards for deliberative public engagement, notably by (a) providing public reasons for major policy and program decisions; (b) creating or deepening channels for citizens (or civil society organizations) to advance input on major policy and program decisions, and to voice concerns about existing policies (see Section 4.5); (c) giving timely formal response to expressed concerns; and (d) enabling citizens to provide input into review of national governments' compliance with their obligations under the organization (e.g., progress toward global climate change targets).

National governments would still have primary responsibility for representing their citizens' concerns, but supplementary avenues for direct transmission and accountability between citizens and IOs (pioneered by individual complaint mechanisms under UN human rights treaties) are nevertheless important. This is especially true where governments lack sufficient capacity or willingness to represent their citizens' interests in inclusive fashion. Such standards could draw on and extend the Convention on Access to Information, Public Participation in Decision-Making and Access to Justice in Environmental Matters (the Aarhus Convention), or the United Nations Development Programme's (UNDP) Stakeholder Response Mechanism, a non-judicial avenue for individuals and groups affected by UNDP activities to resolve disputes.

## 3.3 Regimes and Regime Complexes

International relations scholars have long recognized the importance of regimes in global governance. A regime is a set of accepted principles, norms, and rules for policymaking, operating in a functional issue area such as trade, intellectual property rights, biodiversity, or finance (Krasner 1983). Both states and civil society operate within regimes, supporting and contesting the underlying "principles, norms, and rules" in complex ways. Networks of actors within and across regimes are therefore vital in understanding how regimes emerge and change over time.

Neorealist, liberal, and constructivist theories offer alternative explanations of why regimes were created and sustained. Neorealists focus on how powerful actors use regimes to consolidate and promote their own power, liberals argue that regimes stabilize rules and create incentives for actors to cooperate over time, while constructivists stress the norms that sustain different regimes. Whatever the reason regimes exist, scholars widely agree that the relationships and norms upon which regimes are built enable trust, cooperation, and communication across states and other actors, thus providing some of the preconditions for deliberation. A central empirical development ushered in by regime theory – though reflecting earlier work on complex interdependence in the international system by Keohane and Nye (1977) – pointed to the ways in which myriad actors contributed to the operation and day-to-day affairs of different issue areas. These actors included states, international organizations, and nongovernmental organizations (NGOs).

Over the past two decades, the concept of international regimes has become somewhat less fashionable. Today, the term "regime complex" is more common. A regime complex is "an array of partially overlapping and nonhierarchical institutions governing a particular issue-area" (Raustiala and Victor 2004:

279). Both concepts can be subsumed under global governance. The idea of regime complexes captures something important about the way regimes – with commonly accepted norms and rules – are evolving and sometimes breaking down, as issue areas splinter when new actors emerge, creating different rules reflecting varied normative visions.

Raustiala and Victor (2004) showed that regime complexes were not just increasingly dense but also contained legal inconsistencies and overlapped in complicated and nonhierarchical ways with other regime complexes. Since this seminal work, most issue areas – climate change, plant genetic resources, nuclear proliferation, human rights, trade, and so on – have been described as governed by regime complexes. This concept was further fleshed out by Keohane and Victor (2011), who argued that regime complexes resemble polycentric governance systems in which multiple and overlapping sets of institutions, participants, and mechanisms exist to foster cooperation.

Does this shift toward regime complexity (and thus global governance more broadly) facilitate deliberative democratization? Some scholars are skeptical. Alter and Meunier (2009) and Drezner (2009) argue that fragmented international rules muddle the obligations that different actors hold, thus allowing those actors to abrogate their duties. These scholars claim that this abrogation enables powerful actors, who are also less constrained by legal obligations, to leverage material and cognitive resources to satisfy their preferences. This scenario – which foregrounds power – would undermine deliberation. Forum shopping enables powerful countries to pick the institutional venue that will best further their interests.

However, there are three reasons for deliberative democrats to be more positive. First, in terms of inclusion, regime complexes enable the rise of new actors and their ideas in the governance landscape. Second, related to authentic deliberation, the existence of multiple and overlapping legal jurisdictions often means that "weaker" actors can ignore the demands of "stronger" actors, forcing the latter to rely on argument and persuasion instead of coercion to induce change and generate compliance. This means that power sometimes recedes into the background, opening space for deliberation. Moreover, the lack of hegemons means that actors have to rely upon mutual understanding to build trust. Third, when it comes to consequentiality, because regime complexes open spaces for weaker actors to contest and revise rules, different actors gain the chance to change rules through building relationships and advancing new arguments.

Empirically, Kuyper (2014) demonstrates that because they work largely through persuasion across key actors and institutions, regime complexes are promising sites for deliberative democratization. Kuyper shows that deliberation can be promoted both in negotiations between rule-makers (states and international organizations) and in the relationships between rule-makers and rule-takers (such as corporations, advocacy groups, and even individuals). This can lead to inclusive and authentic deliberation. In a concrete application to the intellectual property rights regime complex, Muzaka (2010) shows that weaker actors pushed out of rule-making in the WTO could reframe their arguments and use the World Intellectual Property Organization (WIPO) to advance their goals. This highlights the importance of argumentation and building mutual understanding between otherwise disadvantaged actors. Finally, the work of Hoffmann (2011) on climate governance shows that regime complexity enables actors, either in isolation or in combination, to experiment with policy solutions to governance problems in innovative ways.

These theoretical and empirical points highlight the potential that regime complexes have for deliberative democracy. While scholars are right to point out that these arrangements can enable powerful actors to get their way, all governance systems will contain some imbalances. The important question is then: How do regime complexes open up pathways and avenues to promote deliberative democratization? We have suggested that the conditions of regime complexity open space for the inclusion of new actors, induce actors to rely on persuasion to get their points across, and facilitate local experiments and adaptations. Though there are no guarantees, regime complexes allow actors to cooperate in ways that advance deliberative democratic ideals.

## 3.4 Global Constitutionalism and Legal Pluralism

International regime complexes provide fertile terrain for deliberative global governance. However, some scholars argue that complex forms of global governance should give way to more centralized orders that can limit power imbalances and thus promote democratization. These two positions mirror debates between global legal pluralists (such as Berman 2006) and global constitutionalists (such as Peters 2009) in the field of international law.

Within the nation state, a constitution is the standard device to distribute power and prevent its abuse. Constitutions delimit the power of government officials and provide individuals with the rights necessary to exercise democratic agency. Cosmopolitan thinkers (and, at an extreme, proponents of a world state such as Cabrera 2004) believe something similar could apply at the global level to curtail transnational abuses of power and democratically empower citizens. If it did apply, extending deliberative principles to the process of constitution-writing would be very straightforward; historically, such principles do tend to come to the fore during constitution-making (Elster 1998). There is a strong constitutionalist strand in the field of deliberative democracy, for which constitutions make possible the conditions for public deliberation, while themselves being the product of deliberative processes in both their establishment and amendment.

However, solidifying a global constitutional order could have deliberative costs. Historically, hegemons have been able to take advantage of large-scale institutional shifts to cement their power (Ikenberry 2009). Attempts to build a global constitution could well be seized upon by these powerful actors. Moreover, while most countries now have constitutions, they differ greatly in form and content; such diversity means it may be harder to secure universal agreement on a global constitution than was the case for the (more limited) UN Charter.

In contrast, and consistent with what we have said about regime complexes, global pluralism celebrates the diversity of international legal arrangements and the different normative positions that are expressed therein. Pluralists accept that globalization fosters inchoate regulatory rules, actors, and processes, and then seeks to harness the benefits of the overlapping legal authorities (Berman 2006). Krisch (2010) argues that pluralism – much more than constitutionalism – provides scope for democratic values of deliberation and revisability to take hold in global governance. Existing pluralist arrangements can be democratized through deliberative means.

Some middle ground between constitutionalism and pluralism may be found as it is possible to think not of an overarching global constitution but rather in terms of constitutions that apply to specific institutions. Compliance with these constitutions could be overseen by courts or tribunals using deliberative principles to rule against abuses of power. In this light, the WTO and WIPO could be seen as having competing constitutions, and weaker actors could seek out the one that offered them greater democratic protections, thus helping gradually to ratchet up deliberative democratic procedures across institutions. We would still caution against any more comprehensive global constitutionalism and against excessive rigidity in any constitution if it impedes the inclusive deliberative reconstruction we have described.

## 3.5 Governance Networks

A governance network is a cooperative horizontal arrangement with informal aspects encompassing multiple actors – some of which can be units of government – that contributes to public ends. At the national level, network governance has emerged as a response to the "hollowing out" of the state induced by neoliberalism, i.e., the decline in expertise and capacity among bureaucrats to design and deliver policy (Rhodes 1997). Networks can exist on anything from health care to energy policy. While states have hollowed, NGOs have proliferated, often possessing considerable knowledge and expertise.

At the international level, there is no state to hollow. Given the variable reach of international organizations, and the fragmentation of regimes into regime complexes discussed previously, there are substantial opportunities for networks involving NGOs, national government departments, subnational governments, corporations, experts, and others to fill gaps and exercise authority. Network governance may also be an adaptive response to the complexity of problems. Though he does not use the terminology, Hoffmann (2011) documents the rise of numerous networked arrangements in transnational climate governance, which he interprets as a response to the failure of the multilateral UN Framework Convention on Climate Change (UNFCCC) to make significant progress. Examples range from the information sharing of the ICLEI cities network to voluntary carbon markets.

There are sharp disagreements about whether network governance will deliver good outcomes. Stoker (2006) maintains that the increasing openness of formal institutions to this informal realm will draw political disputes closer to bureaucracy, such that the diverse consequences of policy can be better anticipated. But there is a dark side to network governance. Lowi (1999) suggests that networks involve a wholesale undemocratic loss of public authority, as power resides in unaccountable places (the Forest Stewardship Council has developed formal accountability, but only to its members). Lowi's view is consistent with old concerns about the disasters that accompany the capture of policy by special interests (see Olson 1982 on its role in the decline of nations). But if network governance is indeed an adaptive response to complexity, the question is how to make the best of it in deliberative and democratic terms.

Those who participate in network governance do not represent geographical constituencies, are not elected, are rarely formally authorized, and are accountable only if they so choose. However, networks can still be assessed according to deliberative and democratic principles. Networks are coordinated by language and work by persuasion rather than command (because there is no sovereign authority) or bargaining (because unhappy parties can easily exit). Networks can be evaluated in terms of whether they are inclusive of the relevant range of actors, views, and discourses; whether their communications are public, well-justified in terms of relevant values, and capable of inducing reflection; and whether they strive to forge principles that could be supported by all those they affect. There is no guarantee that networks will communicate in these terms and, because much of their communication is conducted in private, it can be hard to tell.

Existing deliberative assessments of networks in transnational climate governance (such as the Climate Technology Initiative's Private Finance Advisory Network) suggest that they fall far short of deliberative ideals, and not just on publicity. The key problem is lack of participation on the part of civil society or other potentially critical actors that could hold the power exercised in and by the network to account (Stevenson and Dryzek 2014: 86–119). In practice, these networks are dominated by market-friendly discourse. Yet it would be asking a lot of social movements and activists, whose resources are already stretched, to take on the critical role in specific networks (a role which would probably be resisted anyway). The solution is to establish deliberative accountability from the network to a multilateral body such as the UNFCCC, which in turn should be more accountable to civil society, which therefore only need concentrate its attention on the UNFCCC – not every network (Stevenson and Dryzek 2014: 193–195).

The UNFCCC and other multilateral bodies have shown some interest in actively steering networks, rather than just allowing networks to emerge in response to governance lacunae. International organizations have tried to "orchestrate" networks, to constitute them in a desirable form and direct their efforts to justifiable ends (Abbott and Snidal 2010). As it stands, orchestration mostly involves the international organizations enlisting NGOs (and sometimes corporations and subnational governments) to exert pressure on states and corporations to meet their commitments (such as reducing greenhouse gas emissions). However, orchestration could create deliberative space inasmuch as it gives NGOs and other actors leverage to ask for accountability from the international organization in exchange for their assistance, which would enable a more critical role. The ensuing structure could then be informed by deliberative principles of publicity, inclusion of those affected (Hendriks 2008), justification, and accountability.

## 3.6 Scientific Assessments

Assessing the state of scientific (and other forms of) knowledge is necessary for addressing many complex global problems. Assessments of this kind are especially prominent in governing global environmental problems such as climate change and ozone depletion, which require not only a sophisticated understanding of how the Earth's self-regulatory systems work but also an appreciation of how those problems affect different communities across the world. Such assessments are also essential for making progress on problems ranging from health pandemics to global food insecurity.

The best-known assessment body of this kind is the Intergovernmental Panel on Climate Change (IPCC), which has proven indispensable in strengthening the evidentiary base for action to reduce global greenhouse gas emissions and adapt to a changing climate. The IPCC was partly inspired by the successes of early international scientific efforts, especially those of the Global Ozone Research and Monitoring Project, which informed the drafting and adoption of the Montreal Protocol and subsequent amendments to its parent treaty, the Vienna Convention (Haas 1992; NASA et al. 1986).

Assessment bodies may often feature good deliberation internally, mainly because scientists must reach out to those in different disciplines who do not understand their own specialist language (see Norgaard 2008 on the Millennium Ecosystem Assessment). However, they have been criticized from various quarters. The fiercest criticism of the IPCC has come from climate change deniers and others bent on hobbling progress on climate policy, but others have delivered more measured critiques over its internal operations as well as its engagement with the public.

The IPCC has moved to address some of these concerns by explaining more transparently how it deals with uncertainty over the current state of knowledge and by investing more in public communication. However, these changed practices have not necessarily led to greater success in convincing publics and politicians. In response, Moser and Dilling (2011) argue for a new approach to the engagement of science and society. Such an approach would be reciprocal rather than one-way, involving experts, advocates, and members of the public and civil society, in which experts can respond to lay concerns. Others call for a pluralist approach to assessing knowledge in which the physical sciences are less dominant and there is more space for the social sciences and humanities, as well as for knowledge held by Indigenous peoples and local communities (Beck et al. 2014). Different sorts of knowledge claims have to be reconciled; deliberation is an effective means of doing so.

The Intergovernmental Science-Policy Platform on Biodiversity and Ecosystem Services (IPBES; formed in 2012, over twenty years after the IPCC's origins in 1988) has taken significant steps toward including different forms of knowledge. A distinct focus of its work has been to engage Indigenous peoples and local communities who occupy much of the world's highly biodiverse areas and often have an unparalleled understanding of how species are responding to environmental change. However, numerous practical and discursive obstacles remain to ensuring that representatives of these groups can participate meaningfully in what to many remains a distant scholarly exercise.

A deliberative approach would deepen reciprocal engagement across experts and society. Strategies could include: (i) a more inclusive approach to setting priorities for global assessments, for example by giving greater voice to civil society organizations in addition to national delegations; (ii) actively seeking out citizen engagement on how global risks manifest and are perceived at local levels (for example, through transnational citizens' juries and mini-publics discussed in Section 4.3); (iii) assessing knowledge about the values that people hold (especially if they have an opportunity to reflect on those values) which bear on global risks (e.g., the importance that people ascribe to conserving nature, or their perceptions of risks associated with different technologies for combating climate change); and (iv) synthesizing and putting into practice knowledge about effective ways of communicating the findings of expert assessments to citizens and policymakers.

Deliberative knowledge assessments could extend well beyond environmental problems to contentious policy issues such as the global arms trade, people trafficking, and refugee flows. Knowledge assessments might usefully form deliberative links with policy-oriented bodies (such as the UNFCCC) that have a mandate to generate recommendations for action or to reach decisions. Other forms of assessment could move beyond synthesizing existing knowledge to generating new knowledge to inform collective action, particularly where knowledge is held by those marginalized from existing decision-making processes. A pioneering example here is the World Bank's "Voices of the Poor" project, which conducted 40,000 participatory poverty assessments to understand how people in 50 countries experience poverty and well-being (Narayan et al. 2000).

We have shown that it is possible to think in terms of the deliberative democratization of existing institutions and practices. To the extent this is done, it may set the scene for more substantial innovation, to which we now turn.

## 4 Establishing New Institutions

In thinking about establishing new institutions, it is generally undesirable simply to scale up to the global level liberal democratic models and institutions, such as parliaments, that were developed in the West. It is not possible (nor desirable) to avoid all cultural specificity in institutional proposals, but its adverse forms can be minimized.

## 4.1 A Deliberative Global Citizens' Assembly

To help reduce the global democratic deficit, the idea of a Deliberative Global Citizens' Assembly (DGCA) was proposed by Dryzek, Bächtiger, and Milewicz (2011) as a feasible and effective alternative to utopian proposals for an elected global parliament (the dismal experience of elections to the European Parliament hardly inspires optimism for the latter). There is already sufficient practical knowledge to create an effective DGCA, building on experiences with citizens' assemblies in several countries. Some deliberative practices (such as deliberative polls) that began at local or national levels have already been extended transnationally.

The DGCA might be composed of around 750 representatives, drawn from all 193 UN member states (plus Palestine). (For comparison, the European Parliament has 751 members and the National People's Congress in China has around 3,000 members.) There are four main organizational issues to consider: how representation might be apportioned in the DGCA; how the members might be chosen; how its processes might function; and what principal functions the DGCA might serve.

*Apportionment.* The DGCA could employ a system of representation according to population. This might mean combining groups of small states (such as Pacific island states) to select one representative. Alternatively, each state would be guaranteed one representative. Then, additional seats would be allotted, roughly proportional to population size. Following this method, China, for instance, could expect to hold roughly 19 percent of the seats in the assembly, while the United States could expect roughly 4 percent. Meanwhile, Maldives could expect just one seat.

*Selecting the DGCA's members.* Once it is known how many seats each state is allocated, the next task is to select the members. Some might think that, as a matter of democratic choice, each state (even undemocratic ones) should select its own representatives according to its own preferred criteria. The members might, then, be elected officials or appointed cabinet members from the respective states, prominent scientists or other public intellectuals nominated by their own states, citizens selected through random selection, or others. However, the DGCA should be thought of as a global assembly for the citizens of the world rather than the "representatives" of its nations. Correspondingly, we suggest that the DGCA's members should all be selected through stratified random sampling (stratification is a check that relevant demographic categories are represented). This condition could be stipulated in the assembly's rules and regulations or its founding constitution. The selection might be coordinated by the United Nations or by DGCA staff at the global level. Alternatively, it might be performed by each state itself (with due regard to the danger of states manipulating selection to yield people compliant with the government's interests). Either way, selection ought to ensure a representative spread of social characteristics such as income, education, and gender at the global level – though achieving such a spread will be impossible *within* countries where the numbers of delegates is low (as few as one).

The acceptance rate for invitations to citizens to participate in demanding national or subnational deliberations currently varies from about 5 percent to about 35 percent. The latter figure was achieved for the Australian Citizens' Parliament (Hartz-Karp et al. 2010), which demonstrates it is possible to get people to say "yes" by framing the invitation in dignified terms – as a privilege and a matter of good citizenship – rather than as a burden.

An alternative membership model might also be considered for the DGCA: a majority of members could be lay citizens, while a minority could be politicians. This worked well in Ireland's Constitutional Convention held in 2012–2014 and might be more palatable to existing power-holders at the global level.

*Processes.* For the purposes of deliberation, the DGCA could be broken down into groups of around twenty people (while avoiding divisions based on country or region). The multilingual global context would be challenging, though experience from the EU-wide Europolis deliberative opinion poll, conducted in 2009, shows that simultaneous translation can support robust deliberation. Trained facilitators should help to ensure deliberative quality in the small groups. Positions and considerations developed in these small groups could then be fed into plenary sessions. The DGCA could vote or seek consensus on proposals. Just as important, however, would be the generation of ideas and the sorting of good from bad arguments for and against proposals.

There is compelling evidence that, given the right setting and enough time, lay citizens can be effective, competent, and judicious deliberators – irrespective of their level of education (see, for example, Rao and Sanyal 2010 on citizen deliberation in South India). And if any problems on this score are anticipated, it is always possible to run capacity-building exercises for participants whose confidence might need a boost.

Typically, assemblies of lay citizens prove especially good at listening to arguments, judiciously evaluating information, reflecting upon the merits of policy proposals, and reaching well-thought-out conclusions and well-reasoned positions. There is evidence that deliberating citizens prioritize common interests (such as ecological integrity) as opposed to moneyed special interests (Fishkin 2009: 109 and 142; Smith 2009: 94). Similar results could be expected from a well-organized DGCA.

*The DGCA's Functions.* Maximally, the DGCA could be a general-purpose chamber passing resolutions with standing in international law, acting as a second chamber alongside the UN General Assembly. In this way, the DGCA would operate similarly to the upper houses that exist in many parliamentary democracies. Extensive empirical research indicates that bodies of lay citizens are especially good at the task of reflecting upon the merits of different arguments and proposals (in the same way that juries of citizens in criminal cases reflect upon the relative strength of the cases made by advocates for the two sides). The DGCA could be consultative or it could have more bite, if, for example, it was able to reverse a vote passed by the other chamber. The DGCA could conceivably have a representative on the UNSC. As a citizen body, the DGCA could add legitimacy and so power to the General Assembly.

A general-purpose DGCA is perhaps unlikely in the foreseeable future. More feasibly, an Assembly could initially be constituted to address one issue – such as priorities for global poverty reduction, or global cooperation on gender equality or climate change response – in conjunction with multilateral negotiations or international organizations. To date, most citizens' assemblies within states have been on specific issues such as electoral system reform (in Canada) or access to abortion (in Ireland). The Belgian G1000 had a more open agenda but converged on three issues: immigration, wealth distribution, and social security. Issue-specific and time-limited assemblies have the advantage that their participants are perhaps less likely to become professionalized and so take on the characteristics of politicians or international bureaucrats, or be ripe targets for lobbyists seeking to exchange favors. So a general-purpose DGCA would not necessarily be more desirable, though it would probably have a higher profile than any issue-specific body. Should issue-specific DGCAs perform well, that could add to the case for an all-purpose chamber.

Like any substantial institutional innovation, a DGCA could face serious opposition from powerful actors – though as we have indicated, opposition could likely be ameliorated by having a minority of politicians in the Assembly. In addition, the remit of the DGCA could be constructed so as to avoid undermining the sovereignty of states. At the very least, a DGCA would face fewer obstacles than an elected global parliament. Not being elected, the assembly would not appear to be a competitor to the US Congress, hence would be less likely to face opposition from Americans who find any authority above the US constitution unpalatable. And neither would the DGCA require a country such as China to institute national elections. Of course, there may be opposition from other quarters: for instance, from global industries (e.g., the oil industry) worried about the implications of meaningful and effective cooperation in response to global challenges (e.g., global climate change). Still, there is little reason to think the DGCA is beyond the realm of practical possibility. International organizations in search of the enhanced legitimacy that opening up to transnational inputs provides might support a DGCA. There is already ample experience with large-scale deliberations involving hundreds or even thousands of people – at local, regional, national, and even international levels.

## 4.2 Nested Forums

Deliberation about pressing global issues could also be organized in a system of nested forums stretching from the local to the global level, inspired by Shalom's (2005) "Parpolity" proposal for nested councils. We refer to forums rather than councils to stress that they should not be units of government. The idea is to link conversations about pressing global problems that occur at the global level to conversations about these same issues at more proximate scales – all the way down to the local level. This linkage would reflect the fact that some global problems (such as climate change) have multiple local causes and manifestations. These forums could – at the top of the "nesting" – feed into a DGCA or other substantive global body (such as the UN General Assembly or WTO).

Suppose each local forum has 25 members. Each would nominate (or randomly select from willing participants) a delegate to a second-level forum, also composed of 25 delegates. Delegates at the second level would try to reflect the views of the respective forums they come from but would not be mandated to follow the views of their "constituents" (because they need to be open to persuasion by other participants). Second-level forums would in turn choose delegates to a third level, and so forth. Ideally, the members of the higher-level forums would frequently return to the forums for which they are delegates, reporting on deliberations at the higher level, creating organic links between the levels, strengthening accountability and thus generating legitimacy for the pyramid of nested forums.

Forums at higher levels could meet in person or virtually. Theoretically, seven layers of 25-person forums would be enough to cover the world's population aged 15 and above; six layers of 43-person forums would suffice as well. Practically, coverage would be patchy, but the intent is to provide one means for citizen participation in global governance, not the only means. While the focus would be on global issues, forum discussions would generate ideas for action at lower levels too. After all, ideas for action "at the global level" will require action at more proximate levels as well (e.g., strategies for climate change response involve changes in local patterns of consumption and production). Presumably, then, forum discussions will generate ideas that stimulate more immediate action at these lower levels as well. The nested forums would not be endowed with decision-making authority, hence they should not threaten the authority of states.

In the pyramid of nested forums, ideas and concrete proposals for action would flow upwards from the lowest to the highest level – and downwards from the highest to the lowest. Following our earlier proposal, suppose, for example, that the DGCA is tasked with addressing global cooperation on gender equality.

The Assembly could begin with several thematic priorities (say, violence against women, sexual harassment, and women in higher education) and some broad suggestions about strategies for addressing the most pressing problems in those areas. Like legislatures, the DGCA should have paid, full-time staff members who assist members in discharging their duties. The staff could, for instance, help members to identify potential thematic priorities; generate information on existing strategies for addressing the major problems in the priority areas; and, in conjunction with the member(s) from their respective state, generate further ideas for action. These ideas and proposals could be fed into the initial deliberations at the DGCA level – which might be broadcast, so that all of the nested forums start their own deliberations from the same baseline.

DGCA staff could also provide the forums with briefing materials. These might provide an explanation of how and why the thematic priorities were selected, and document the ideas and proposals that were fed into the initial deliberations at the DGCA level. The forums would be free to create their own informational materials as well – and to consult with whatever local, regional, national, or international experts or organizations they choose. Likewise, the forums would be free to design principles to govern their own interactions, to "fit" the cultures of those who compose the forums. Some communities may value consensus of the sort Hébert (2018: 102–105, 108) sees in much Indigenous deliberation; others might be open to more robust differences. Experience suggests that when participants do craft principles for their own dialogues, they generally converge on ones that are consistent with deliberative democracy (respectful listening, turn-taking, no ad hominem arguments, etc.).

In any case, the deliberations would then go up the pyramid as suggested. More specifically, each of the lowest-level forums might be asked to generate (say) up to five proposals for action in each of the priority areas. Starting from these proposals, the next level would distil five proposals to go forward, and so forth, all the way to the top. The five proposals distilled at the top in each area would then be submitted to the DGCA for consideration and concrete legislative action. A record of the proposals for action generated by the forums at each level, and their accompanying justifications, could be made available to the DGCA and broader public. A searchable database could be created to track the ideas generated by the forums at each level, facilitating idea-exchanges between the levels and with the broader public. Approval voting (in which voters can register their approval for as many or as few options as they like) might then be used to gauge support for the final DGCA proposals; all participants from each level could participate in a nonbinding vote on the proposals. In this way, the DGCA, an assembly for the citizens of the world, would have its finger on the pulse of each level of nested forums – documenting the major concerns and strategies for action in each of the priority areas and assessing the approval with which the "nested forum public" regards the DGCA's own proposed actions.

This proposal may seem fanciful. However, some transnational practices already involve "nesting." Consider the 2009 European Citizens' Consultations (Bevir and Bowman 2011: 180). Citizens first visited an online portal to discuss, debate, and relay ideas about EU policy options. These ideas were fed into national consultations that took place in all 27 member states. Over three weekends, hundreds of participants at each of these events (a total of 1,600 citizens chosen through random selection) worked to generate ten proposals for action at the EU level. The participants subsequently voted on the recommendations generated by the national events, thus creating a list of the top 15 recommendations. Approximately 150 of the participants then went to Brussels to discuss these recommendations and submit them to EU policymakers.

Nesting can be conceptualized as a form of civil society involvement in global governance, as well as a set of formal institutions. Stevenson (2013) advocates "nested public spheres" as a solution to a pervasive problem in the governance of climate technologies, where global decisions made (for example) by the Clean Technology Fund (CTF) can be insensitive to their local impacts on both social structure and gender relations. Required here is not just local input into local investment plans but also a challenge to the dominant sustainability discourse that conditions the CTF's global operations, one which fails to recognize class and gender as relevant categories. This kind of challenge ought to build on local experiences, and once established inform local implementation. Again, learning goes in both directions between the local and the global. The kind of learning that Stevenson describes, and its critical function in relation to established discourses and policies, is the stuff of social movements and civil society, though it can also play a role in governance structures.

## 4.3 Transnational Citizens' Juries and Mini-publics

Thousands of citizens' juries and related kinds of "mini-publics" have been implemented successfully in countries ranging from Mali and Denmark to India and China (Grönlund, Bächtiger, and Setälä 2014). The basic idea involves convening a small group of citizens through stratified sampling (random sampling alone does not capture the variety of relevant social characteristics with small numbers) to deliberate and produce recommendations. Citizens' juries and similar designs generally involve 15–25 people; citizens' assemblies have been up to 300 people. There are exercises that involve several thousand participants, but these stretch the definition of mini-public by welcoming anyone who wants to turn up.

Citizens' juries aim to create a microcosm of the community (Crosby and Nethercut 2005) in terms of age, gender, educational level, race, and geographic location of residency. Participants usually receive a modest daily stipend and expenses. A citizens' jury is small enough not to need subdivision into smaller deliberating groups (though this is sometimes done). An advisory committee, representing a broad range of interested actors, can oversee the process.

In all mini-publics, facilitators promote equality and civility among participants (Bevir and Bowman 2011: 179). It is standard in mini-publics for facilitators to remain neutral; to not impart information; to support broad participation; and to refrain from promoting consensus among the participants or any restrictions (beyond civility) on what participants can say or on the kind of speech they can use. So participants can tell stories rather than rely only on arguments and do not have to restrict their speech to appeals to the common good. It is possible for the citizens to participate at the outset in the design of the principles that will govern their interactions. As noted in our earlier discussion of nested forums, participants generally converge on principles consistent with deliberative democracy. Expert witnesses and sometimes advocates for different sides of an issue make presentations and answer participants' questions, but do not participate in the participants' deliberations. A citizens' jury typically concludes with a report and recommendations, though sometimes (as in citizens' panels convened in some US states to inform referendums) the main task is to assess the strength of the arguments on each side of the issue.

Ratner and Goodin (2011) argue that citizens' juries, drawn from many countries, could be used to determine the content of *jus cogens* – peremptory norms of international law that no treaty can override, such as prohibitions on torture and the use of force, and stipulations that the UN Charter should take precedence over other treaties. Baber and Bartlett (2015) have carried out citizens' juries in multiple countries and have shown how they can generate common principles for global action on environmental issues (though each of their juries is drawn from a single country).

Deliberative polling, invented by James Fishkin (1995; 2009), uses random sampling rather than stratified sampling of citizens. Otherwise, it shares several characteristics with citizens' juries and other mini-publics: compensation for participants' time, neutral facilitation of small group discussions to promote civility (but not to restrict storytelling, or insist that appeals must be made to the common good), the provision of balanced background materials, and presentations by experts and advocates. However, deliberative polls differ from most other kinds of mini-publics in that they are polls: the participants do not write a report, or craft recommendations, but instead complete a questionnaire both before and after the event (to ascertain opinion change and knowledge gain).

Deliberative polls also claim statistical representativeness of the larger population in both demographic and (initial) attitudinal terms, so their minimum size must be about 150 participants. Due to their large size, deliberative polls are divided into smaller deliberating groups, which reconvene in plenary sessions involving experts and advocates, who can be questioned by citizen-participants. Unlike conventional polls, which largely capture unreflective opinion, "A deliberative poll attempts to model what the public *would* think, had it a better opportunity to consider the questions at issue" (Fishkin 1995: 162).

Dozens of deliberative polls have been conducted in many countries, on issues ranging from energy policy to immigration to crime to whether a monarchy should be abandoned in favor of a republic (in Australia). Some have been conducted online. In Mongolia, there is now a requirement that any proposal to amend the constitution must be preceded by a deliberative poll (Fishkin 2018: 189).

The first transnational deliberative poll, "Tomorrow's Europe," took place in Brussels in 2007. It involved 362 participants drawn from all 27 EU member states, with simultaneous translation across 23 languages. Participants spent a weekend deliberating social, economic, and political issues relevant to the future of the EU and the 27 states. In 2009 the Europolis deliberative poll was convened in Brussels to deliberate issues such as climate change and immigration. Again, participants were citizens from the 27 member states (though as Smith 2018: 863 points out, this meant the poll considered immigration without any input from undocumented migrants). One can imagine similar events at the global level.

To date, the closest resemblance to a global mini-public can be found in World Wide Views, organized by the Danish Board of Technology (DBT). Like deliberative polling, the process features questionnaires, though only after the event. Participants could also develop their own recommendations. The first World Wide Views was held in 2009, when around 90 citizens in each of 38 countries deliberated the issue of climate change, following a common model (though in practice national organizers tweaked the model) on the same day (Rask, Worthington, and Lammi 2012). The results were presented later that year to the Conference of the Parties of the UNFCCC in Copenhagen. In almost all cases, the 90 citizens favored stronger action on climate change than their governments were then prepared to support. The process has been repeated for biodiversity and again for climate change. World Wide Views is a series of national processes, with no transnational interchange. But there is no reason why (say) two individuals could not be selected from participants in each national event and brought together to deliberate, in parallel to the UN negotiations which the process is designed to influence.

Any such initiative might meet opposition from organized civil society groups, especially those currently receiving privileged access to the United Nations as recognized "major groups." But the challenge here is no different from that generally met successfully within states, where mini-publics often hear from civil society advocates. If a group believes in the power of its own arguments, it should have no problem in making those arguments to a mini-public.

Mini-publics always face the challenge that their findings may not be accepted by a larger citizenry, who have not had the same chance to deliberate. However, there is some evidence that nonparticipants trust mini-publics to do the right thing if they believe the mini-public is composed of "people like us" (see survey evidence in MacKenzie and Warren 2012). Publicity for mini-publics' proceedings (through, for example, television, social media, or a report sent to voters) can help here. However, moments of confidentiality, especially in the shadow of deep division and conflict, may be necessary for people from different sides to build trust – without worrying about whether they will be seen as betraying their communities (Chambers 2004). Of course, any outcomes of *in camera* discussions should subsequently be presented for public validation.

Mini-publics should not be seen as decision-making bodies. Rather, they can serve functions in larger systems of deliberation – such as inducing better large-scale public deliberation, bringing new arguments and ideas to the attention of decision-makers, or embodying reflection that can otherwise be in short supply. We will have more to say about these functions in our later discussion of deliberative systems.

## 4.4 Deliberative Crowdsourcing

Crowdsourcing is a distributed, sometimes collaborative, way to accomplish tasks and solve problems online. It presents a way to leverage the collective intelligence of individuals and communities for the purposes set out in an open call. It can be paid or unpaid. Common kinds of crowdsourcing include idea generation, knowledge search, argumentation (the integration of different perspectives), and microtasking (dividing complex tasks into manageable pieces) (Aitamurto and Landemore 2016: 177). It has been used in areas as diverse as energy system research, journalism, linguistics, astronomy, and genealogical research.

Local, state, and national governments have deployed crowdsourcing in policymaking, involving thousands of citizens. Typically, crowdsourcing is not deliberative. Yet it can become so when accompanied by reasoned interchange among the participants.

Aitamurto and Landemore (2016: 191) speak of "crowdsourced deliberation" as an "open . . . asynchronous, depersonalized, and distributed" kind of online deliberation among self-selected participants in the context of an effort by a government or other organization to open up the policymaking or lawmaking process. They document how crowdsourced deliberation featured in the research and drafting stage of a legislative process in Finland, concerning an off-road traffic law that regulates motorized transportation in the countryside. They found that "despite the lack of clear incentives for deliberation in the crowdsourced process, crowdsourcing functioned as a space for democratic deliberation" (2016: 175). One worry is that self-selected participant pools may generate a limited range of information, views, and arguments, hence low-quality deliberation unrepresentative of the diversity of relevant opinions and perspectives in the larger community of affected interests. Yet, "despite the lack of statistical representativeness among the participants" in the Finnish case, "the deliberative exchanges reflected a diversity of viewpoints and opinions" (2016: 175). Participants were "impressed by the inclusiveness and representativeness of the process in that respect, even if it was remarked that some groups were not represented (e.g., the indigenous Sami people, and people without access to the Internet)" (2016: 191).

Crowdsourced deliberation has also been used in constitution-making in Iceland – though the proposals generated were eventually vetoed by a jealous parliament (Landemore 2015). Crowdsourcing could likewise inform the operations of the deliberative bodies we have proposed, including the DGCA, the nested forums, and the transnational citizens' juries and other mini-publics. In the Iceland case, a mini-public organized the deliberative crowdsourcing.

Recent UN efforts to involve large numbers of people are limited by the fact that they are not deliberative. The MY World survey begun in 2013, in conjunction with the process to produce the SDGs, reached over 7 million people (Gellers 2016), to little discernable effect on the larger process. The "e-discussion" conducted around the same issue at the same time on The World We Want platform was more promising: It enabled individuals to access a trove of relevant information and to contribute to a "global online conversation" (United Nations Development Group 2013: 7). The output of this e-discussion involved selection and synthesis of comments in a summary report, whose impact on the subsequent formation of the SDGs is hard to trace.

In theory, the number of people that could be involved in crowdsourced deliberation is limitless. Aitamurto and Landemore (2016: 192) suggest that innovative technologies and natural language processing could include hundreds of thousands of people in meaningful ways. Crowdsourcing could, say, generate ideas for a global civic education curriculum or for how to finance the United Nation's operations.

## 4.5 A Global Dissent Channel

A global dissent channel would expand the range of meaningful opportunities for people to raise dissenting opinions on key issues with international organizations. This idea builds on the Dissent Channel created within the US Foreign Service in 1971 following internal opposition to the conduct of the Vietnam War. To date, the US channel has only had limited success in triggering reform, but it has served as a pressure valve when diplomats disagree with government policy (Gurman 2011). The channel came to renewed prominence when more than a thousand US diplomats voiced their criticism of President Trump's ban on migration from seven Muslim-majority countries, becoming "one of the broadest protests by American officials against their president's policies" (Gettleman 2017).

A global dissent channel would need to be stronger and broader than the US model. It would be an independent body under UN auspices, to which established and new organizations could subscribe. Although individual organizations could set up their own dissent channels, a single entry point would improve public access, particularly for marginalized communities that face daunting challenges in navigating the United Nation's fragmented institutional landscape. Any individual or organization affected by the practices or policies of a participating international organization would be eligible to submit a complaint (either directly or through a representative). Once complaints are received, decision-makers would be obliged to give a timely and considered response.

Complaints could be submitted either in writing or in formats such as audio or video recordings to ensure access is not restricted to those who are literate. The amount of traffic in the channel could be kept manageable by crowdsourcing dissent, enabling large numbers of affected people to craft a single complaint. To address the possibility of the channel being overwhelmed by organized campaigns or ill-founded but popular ideas, a nonpartisan filter would be necessary, perhaps a mini-public (see Section 4.3). The responsiveness of organizations to opinions submitted through the channel could be monitored and publicized.

A global dissent channel would be a substantial step beyond existing channels for voicing grievances, such as the World Bank's Grievance Redress Service and the Green Climate Fund's Independent Redress Mechanism. Typically, in these channels claims can only be made by people (or their representatives) who are adversely affected by projects funded by the organization. Eligibility does not usually extend to those who wish to express disagreement with the organization's overall priorities or practices. The United Nations also has an Ombudsman service, but this is only available for staff who have employment-related complaints. While a dissent channel would not have the investigative powers of an Ombudsman, it would advance deliberative accountability, requiring decision-makers to give an account of their actions.

## 4.6 Financing New Institutions

Deliberative institutions can be time-consuming and require ample resources. Yet the resources required are generally small in comparison to what is at stake in big decisions and the immense damage that can occur when global governance goes wrong. Thus deliberative processes will more than pay for themselves if they produce more effective and legitimate (so compliance-inducing) decisions along lines we have indicated.

Improving the deliberative quality of existing global governance arrangements – involving, as discussed earlier, multilateral negotiations, international organizations and regimes, governance networks, and scientific assessments would not require much in terms of financial resources, for the required change is mainly in principles and procedures.

Constructing new deliberative bodies (such as a DGCA) requires investment in infrastructure to house deliberative bodies and personnel to manage their operations, and in the development and rollout of technologies to enable people to participate. Financial and capacity-building assistance may be required to enable marginalized groups to participate. The Europolis deliberative poll received half its funding from the European Commission, the remainder from philanthropic foundations. When it coordinated the first World Wide Views, the DBT was funded by the government of Denmark (later the DBT became a private foundation); partner organizations in many of the countries where World Wide Views was conducted also contributed resources.

Citizens' assemblies are no more expensive to run than elected assemblies, and random selection processes are much less expensive than election campaigns. In principle, additional funding could be raised through taxing activities that undermine good deliberation but are hard or undesirable to prohibit outright: for example, public relations or political advertising. In practice, it would be easier to redirect government expenditures that harm the common interests that deliberation is likely to value, such as fossil fuel subsidies that accelerate climate change or agricultural subsidies in wealthy countries that impoverish farmers in developing countries (Franks et al 2018; Mitchell, Käppeli, and Hillebrandt 2017). Similarly, governments could raise taxes on activities that exacerbate global risks, such as coal and oil extraction or financial speculation.

The problem here is that the power to tax and subsidize generally rests with states. While some institutional innovations could be secured even if a single state acts unilaterally (as the World Wide Views experience suggests), others would require a critical mass of states to act. Eventually, it might be possible to reach multilateral agreement on a small levy on global financial transactions (e.g., the Tobin Tax on currency trades) or on greenhouse gas emissions from international transport. Alternatively, states may find common purpose in combating multinational tax avoidance, which would enhance their ability to finance transnational processes (Forstater 2015).

Revenues from initiatives such as these could be used mainly to address global priorities identified through deliberative processes, but a small portion could be used to finance deliberative processes themselves. The UN SDGs provide a useful framework for overall investment priorities: deliberative processes could be funded under Goal 16 ("Promote peaceful and inclusive societies for sustainable development, provide access to justice for all and build effective, accountable and inclusive institutions at all levels"). Global deliberative budgeting processes could draw on extensive experience with participatory budgeting, which originated in Brazil and has since been adopted in many countries (Wampler and Hartz-Karp 2012).

## 4.7 The Feasibility of Institutional Reforms and Innovations

We suggested at the outset that a deliberative approach to global democratization is more feasible than alternative visions that use parliamentary democracy as practiced within liberal states as a model, and certainly more feasible than anything approaching a global social democracy (Hardt and Negri 2001), a world state, or even a global constitution. We now revisit that claim in light of the more detailed institutional proposals we have made. Feasibility is a concern of long standing in discussions of public policy and institutional design (and even professional philosophers now recognize its importance; see Gilabert and Lawford-Smith 2012).

An outcome is feasible if the desired state of affairs is accessible from our current situation (Buchanan 2004), be it in terms of cost (which we just addressed), the probability of key requirements occurring, or the ability of key actors to bring it to fruition. A proposal is feasible if it does not contradict key political, economic/material, or psychological constraints. On all three points, deliberative global governance fares well. The political challenge is the hardest, given the demonstrated ability of powerful states to stifle even modest reforms to global governance. We have shown how current institutional arrangements can be imbued with deliberative governance, meaning that key sites of global governance – multilateral negotiations, international organizations, regime complexes, and governance networks – could all be made more deliberative. Moreover, the new institutions and practices we propose are much more feasible than the leading alternatives proposed by others, such as directly elected assemblies, and much less likely to be opposed by key players such as the US Congress and government of China.

The kinds of bodies we propose have been trialed successfully in national and subnational governments. The thousands of examples include citizens' assemblies in the UK, Canada, and Ireland; citizens' juries in Mali, India, and Australia; deliberative polls in Mongolia, China, and Uganda; deliberative crowdsourcing in Iceland and Finland; and participatory budgeting in Brazil, Peru, and South Africa. These efforts are part of a global movement to put deliberative democracy in practice. Deliberative initiatives have been supported by local, regional, and national governments in many countries (Ireland has been the exemplary national government in the recent past) and by associations such as the International Association for Public Participation. Prominent figures such as Barack Obama have endorsed the idea of deliberative democracy.

There is good psychological evidence from around the globe that lay citizens as well as activists and leaders can be willing and capable deliberators, given the right opportunities, circumstances, and incentives. As we noted in Section 1.2, deliberation is more consistent with the worldwide roots of democracy than is voting (though we are not hostile to voting). In short, the institutions of deliberative global governance are feasible in political, economic, and psychological terms.

## 5 Cultivating Deliberative Civil Society

The well-being of any political system depends not just – or perhaps even mainly – on formal institutions but also on the condition of deliberation in the broader public sphere, which in matters surrounding global governance is commonly termed global civil society. Because it is informal, the overall configuration of global civil society cannot be designed. Yet its specifics can be evaluated and appreciated – and protected through rights to association, communication, and representation.

### 5.1 Global Civil Society

The old idea of civil society became internationalized in a serious way in the wake of the 1989 collapse of communism in Europe and simultaneous

promotion of civil society by South American antiauthoritarian political movements (Kaldor 2003: 586). The practice of global civil society now involves
numerous non-state actors engaging with each other, with states, and with
global governance processes, especially those associated with the United
Nations. The Rio Earth Summit in 1992 is sometimes seen as a landmark in
the evolution of global civil society, as more than two thousand civil society
organizations attended that meeting, though the roots of global civil society go
back at least as far as antislavery movements in the nineteenth century. Many
thousands of NGOs now engage with global governance institutions, whether or
not they have formal consultative status with the United Nations. Civil society
is largely self-organizing and encompasses social movements, the media, individual activists, public intellectuals, and foundations as well as NGOs. Whether
its rise contributes (along with globalization) to the decline of the system of
sovereign states is debatable. Civil society does add additional layers of semi-
institutionalized activity which interacts with, conditions, and sometimes
shapes the behavior of states (Kaldor, 2003). Civil society is not always
deliberative: Exclusionary and racist movements find their home in this realm
too (Chambers and Kopstein, 2001).

Global civil society involves communication, cooperation, representation,
advocacy, persuasion, and the mobilization, transmission, and amplification of
criticism. (It can also involve service delivery such as health care or development
assistance. But we set that role aside to focus on global civil society's potentially
deliberative and democratic role.) Individuals and groups can contribute to and
monitor the decision-making that occurs at the international level and provide
specialized knowledge to such processes. They can also use this knowledge to
evaluate decisions and hold decision-makers to account, particularly by calling on
decision-makers to justify their actions to ever wider audiences. Non-state actors,
as agents of diverse publics, can enhance public scrutiny and oversight and join
public discourse about the "flaws, merits and performance of governance"
(Steffek, 2010: 47). But is global civil society up to the task of democratizing
global governance in any significant way? To do so it needs to be both deliberative
and democratic. First we show how it can be deliberative, then how it can be
democratic. While there are several ways in which global civil society can
facilitate deliberation (for example, in gatherings such as the World Social
Forum to deliberate issues not dealt with adequately in international organizations), we stress macro-level processes involving the engagement of discourses.

## 5.2 The Deliberative Engagement of Discourses

Global civil society is a realm of communication and persuasion. The sheer
volume and diversity of discourses in the global public sphere might seem to

make it a lively place. Examples of such discourses include neoliberalism, human rights, sustainable development, anticorporate globalization, religious fundamentalisms, transparency (in government), and human security. These discourses can also extend into institutions of government (including international organizations), so they are not coterminous with civil society. Indeed, the weakness of formal governmental institutions means that global discourses matter enormously in ordering governance. So, for instance, financial and economic governance have been ordered largely by the discourse of neoliberalism, while environmental governance has been ordered largely by a discourse of sustainable development.

Civil society is a realm in which discourses can be articulated relatively freely – especially those discourses that are critical of the status quo. Historically, just about all discourses that have proven consequential in ordering global governance – including those adopted by dominant institutions – have their origins in civil society. Even neoliberalism had its origins in a movement of scholars, corporate activists, and think tanks (originating with the Mont Pelerin Society, founded in 1947). The case of neoliberalism as eventually embodied in the "Washington Consensus" illustrates the fact that sometimes a single discourse can dominate an area of global affairs, in this case economics and finance. Subsequently, neoliberalism was contested first by anticorporate globalization and its associated social movements, then by economic nationalism as espoused by President Donald Trump and others.

The deliberative health of global civil society depends on discursive multiplicity as opposed to hegemony. So, for example, in global antipoverty policy, relevant discourses include those highlighting individual rights, charity (which emphasizes the agency of the rich), empowerment (which emphasizes the agency of the poor), effective altruism (rational calculation to maximize the good that charity can do), and sustainable development. This is not a matter of "anything goes" in terms of discourses, for the conditions of their engagement ought to involve competent and critical actors, such that some discourses deservedly fall by the wayside (for example, imperialist discourse that speaks of civilizing backward societies has almost died).

Even where there is what looks like a healthy multiplicity of discourses – for example, in global environmental affairs – discourses (and their adherents) can fail to engage one another in effective ways. Discursive enclaves are common. Scientists, radicals, moderates, conservatives, and business interests form their own circles. Now, enclaves are not necessarily pathological echo chambers; they can help disadvantaged groups to sharpen their arguments and build confidence prior to their entry into the larger public sphere. But enclaves can never be the end of the deliberative story; the deliberative virtues of mutual understanding and collective learning, for instance, require that advocates eventually leave their enclaves and engage others. In this light, engagement across different discourses in the public sphere is central to effective deliberation in global civil society. In Section 8.1 we will show how such engagement is generally missing when it comes to global climate governance – and what to do about it.

Engagement across discourses is also crucial when it comes to reducing the potential for violent conflict in the international system. Violent ethnic, national, and religious conflicts are often the product of competing discourses – because discourses create identities, and (at worst) such identities find validation only in the rejection of other identities (such as different religions or ethnicities). Though he does not use the discourses terminology, Huntington's (1996) notion of a "clash of civilizations" involves exactly this kind of dynamic. Its opposite is a deliberative engagement across discourses, across not just those that define or are associated with what Huntington sees as civilizations (such as a liberal human rights discourse, or an illiberal "Asian values" discourse championed by former Singapore Prime Minister Lee Kuan Yew) but also involving those that can be found in more than one "civilization," such as various discourses related to climate governance or development (Dryzek 2006). Informal "track II" back-channel diplomacy, which is low visibility and carried out by non-state actors, often in the context of a deep conflict, can manifest this sort of engagement.

Effective engagement across discourses does help constitute deliberative democracy, but it is important that the (provisional) outcome of that engagement be consequential when it comes to collective decision-making. Success stories in these terms would include the international campaign against landmines (yielding the 1997 Ottawa Convention) and the eventual influence of the antiglobalization movement on the World Bank's practices (Stiglitz 2002: 20). In environmental affairs, the global dominance of shortsighted economic concerns (and their supporting discourses) as well as the weakness of environmental institutions means that consequentiality can be hard to find. However, as we noted in Section 3.5, the turn to orchestration in global governance opens up possibilities here. Because orchestrators (such as an international organization) rely on civil society organizations to exert pressure on states and others, civil society is in a position to ask for influence and accountability in return (though this can leave the dominance of economic discourses and institutions untouched). At the same time, the deliberative health of global civil society depends on public spheres (which it helps constitute) maintaining autonomy and a critical distance from the exercise of formal authority, so as not to become compromised by entanglements with government, to avoid being co-opted, and to maintain the moral authority that is crucial to the power of civil society.

## 5.3 Democratic Global Civil Society: From Accountability to Discursive Representation

Even if global civil society is (sometimes) deliberative, that does not mean it is democratic, in the sense of promoting broad citizen control over governance. Global civil society does not directly engage more than a tiny fraction of the world's people. Moreover, its resources are limited compared to the institutions and actors they are engaging and sometimes competing with, notably national governments and transnational corporations. Critics point out that most NGOs that operate in the international arena are from wealthy Western countries and that those who work for and support such organizations are, in global terms, elites (Omelicheva 2009). And whatever they contribute to governance, NGOs can be just as unaccountable as the institutions they are supposedly holding to account. The rhetorical question "Who elected Oxfam?" (famously asked by *The Economist* in 2000) tries to make the point that NGOs are unaccountable and unrepresentative.

When it comes to accountability, civil society organizations can at least try to be transparent in their motivations, internal governance, and sources of funding (as well as being accountable to their members, for example, by providing venues for members to criticize leaders). When it comes to accountability and representativeness alike, most civil society organizations look much better than the dictatorial states, hegemonic powers, opaque multinational corporations, unresponsive international organizations, oppressive militaries, and secretive financial networks that loom so large in global governance. Organizations such as Greenpeace and Oxfam are generally more highly trusted than are national governments, transnational corporations, and even the formal institutions of global governance. Here, integrity and relative independence from material self-interest are major resources in facilitating moral authority.

This is not to deny the vulnerabilities of civil society to more insidious forces. Corporations routinely fund astroturfing campaigns in civil society. They fund third parties, including global public relations firms, to make arguments and representations on their behalf, giving the impression these concerns derive from some underrepresented or otherwise disadvantaged group (Bienkov, 2012; Walker 2014). Such practices can also involve the spreading of patent misinformation. To a degree, civil society itself is capable of identifying these activities and rooting them out (Oreskes and Conway 2010). However, the risks should not be understated. Corporations and their political agents have become expert at hiding their trails, especially in digital contexts. More critical institutional capacity is required, not only for NGOs, but also for journalists and scientists.

Despite challenges to their role in global governance, the representative claims of NGOs often fare rather well. This holds where NGOs enhance the ability of their claimed constituencies eventually to speak effectively for themselves, and to cultivate their own accountability to these constituencies (Montanaro 2018). These constituency tests would apply most obviously to donor-driven organizations such as Oxfam. Organizations built from the grassroots up are less vulnerable to charges of unrepresentativeness. While many such grassroots organizations operate nationally, few operate transnationally (though see our discussion of La Via Campesina in Section 8.3).

Most discussions about the democratic credentials of global civil society concern the degree to which its actors represent lay citizens. The very question, however, misses the point because it is premised on a confusion between the character and function of representation in different institutional realms. The purpose of global civil society is not to rule. It is rather to influence governance, hold power-holders publicly accountable, and represent concerns (Scholte 2002).

Here the notion of "discursive representation" can be introduced. This notion moves beyond the idea, central to electoral democracy, that the role of political representatives is to represent people. Rather, just as global civil society can be thought of in terms of the engagement of different discourses, so can its actors be conceived of as representatives of those discourses. Global civil society can be thought of as a pattern of discursive representation (Dryzek 2012: 14). In these terms, Amnesty International represents a human rights discourse, the anti-whaling group Sea Shepherd represents a discourse of green radicalism (and international law enforcement), while Oxfam represents antipoverty. Discursive representation works badly if composed of self-appointed elites impervious to challenge or of corporate stooges whose intention is to manipulate the public sphere to secure some self-interested end. But it can work well where it enables comprehensive representation of concerns that otherwise would not be heard, operating at a critical distance from established centers of power, and accountable in deliberative terms to others who share the discourse. Discourses such as neoliberalism, national security, and counter-terror hardly require special representation in these contexts, given that they are well represented by states, existing international bodies, and corporations. In contrast, discourses such as green radicalism and global justice are in dire need of representation from civil society. Discourses such as antipoverty and sustainable development can be endorsed by powerful actors, but often in ways that neutralize the critical bite of the discourse, such that they still need effective representation from civil society.

In short, global civil society should not be evaluated as if it were a democracy in itself (deliberative or otherwise). Instead, it should be seen as a vital ingredient of the democratization of global governance – taking its place along-side other elements in a deliberative system, whose character and connections we will now set out.

## 6 Putting It All Together: A Global Deliberative System

It is unrealistic to impose the full burden of legitimate and effective global governance on any single institution or practice. Instead, that burden can be distributed in deliberative systems linking institutions and more informal practices, especially those in global civil society.

Recent deliberative democratic theory has seen a "systemic turn" that seeks to illuminate how deliberative systems function in practice – and how they can work better in terms of both democratic values and problem-solving effectiveness (Dryzek 2010; Mansbridge et al. 2012). Deliberative systems operate at multiple levels, ranging from local communities and national polities to the world at large. Some systems may be issue-specific (e.g., on gender equality or migration) while others may be defined by their geographic or jurisdictional scope (e.g., a deliberative system for governing a small island state, or the system for global governance that we elaborate here). Smaller deliberative systems may be nested within larger ones.

Most of the work that has appeared on deliberative systems to date looks at national and subnational levels (e.g., Parkinson and Mansbridge 2012; Barvosa 2018). One of the few works to take a global perspective is Stevenson and Dryzek (2014), which evaluates the deliberative system for global climate governance and explores how it could be improved. The account presented here builds on this work and expands it to global governance more broadly.

## 6.1 Components of a Global Deliberative System

Any system features differentiated yet linked components that can be interpreted and evaluated in terms of some common purpose. For deliberative systems, those common purposes include democracy, justice, and effective resolution of common problems. While related to other concepts such as governance systems or policy systems, a deliberative systems approach foregrounds how different components can interact to yield deliberative and democratic system-level qualities.

A deliberative system (illustrated in Figure 1) consists of:

- *Empowered space* where authoritative collective decisions are produced. There can be a division of institutional labor within empowered space.

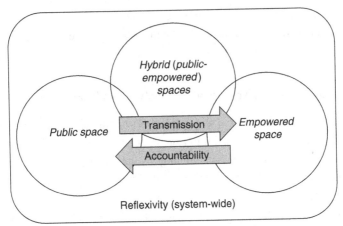

**Figure 1** Components of a deliberative system

- *Public space* where ideas and discourses are generated and engage with one another, especially in civil society.
- *Hybrid spaces* sharing characteristics of both empowered and public space (for example, forums for dialogue between government and civil society, and networks of public and private actors).
- *Transmission* of influence from public space to empowered space, through information, argument, rhetoric, or demonstration.
- *Accountability* of empowered space to public space.
- *Reflexivity*: the capacity of a system to examine and where necessary change itself, including a capacity for *meta-deliberation* (that is, deliberation about the system's own deliberative qualities).

What is important are the deliberative and democratic qualities of the system as a whole – not just its component parts. When a deliberative system works well, it can compensate for the deficiencies of individual parts and amplify their strengths. The component parts can specialize. So the formation of citizen preferences, along with free, open, and inclusive deliberation, and meaningful engagement across discourses, can be sought first in public space (see Section 5.2). Consequential deliberation directed at specific global problems should be sought first in empowered space (which can feature multilateral bodies, or governance networks, or regimes).

The capacities and connectedness of public and empowered space may vary widely across and within areas of global governance. In climate governance, Stevenson and Dryzek (2014) find that public space around UNFCCC negotiations is vibrant but only marginally influential, while public space around networked climate governance (including climate funds and voluntary carbon markets) is far smaller and much less capable of holding networked actors to account. Whereas public space is more established around multilateral meetings on human rights and the environment, civil society generally has far less access in other areas, particularly security and finance (Sommerer and Tallberg 2017).

## 6.2 Linkages in a Deliberative System

The linkages between parts of a deliberative system are crucial. These linkages can be intrinsically deliberative – for example, when accountability involves an interchange between international negotiators and civil society groups. But they need not be – for example, activist protests may get items on the agenda and transmit concerns that were otherwise ignored.

Though the specifics can vary across governance areas, linkages can involve many of the institutions and practices we have discussed in previous sections, including:

- *Meaningful engagement* across discourses in public space, to transcend the enclaves within which discourses often operate in civil society.
- *Discursive representation* (by activists and advocates) to transmit concerns from public space to empowered space.
- *Crowdsourcing* that draws on the wisdom of individuals, transmitted to mini-publics, international organizations, or multilateral negotiations.
- For issues with an important scientific aspect, *mini-publics* (and other bodies) can engage expert assessments in deliberative fashion.
- *Deliberative accountability mechanisms* running from any formally established body (be it the DGCA, a mini-public, or a multilateral negotiation) to public space.

Figure 2 shows how these elements can be combined into a coherent global system.

Discursive representation and crowdsourcing are likely to be dominated by more active and engaged people. In contrast, the nested forums we described are constructed from a much broader base and so are quite likely to transmit different sorts of concerns. Reflection on what various advocates have to say is the specific task of the citizen bodies we have described, notably the DGCA. The DGCA and mini-publics can secure public trust precisely because they are composed of people whose characteristics reflect those of broader publics.

Deliberative systems thinking shows how to redeem the promise of polycentric governance as advocated prominently by Ostrom (2010; see also Galaz et al. 2012). Polycentrism encompasses initiatives at multiple levels ranging from public–private partnerships to local government to cooperative resource management. The problem with polycentrism is that it does not

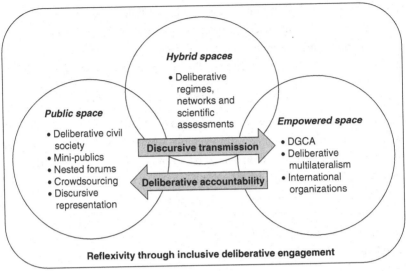

**Figure 2** A global deliberative system

necessarily have anything to coordinate disparate governance efforts and ensure they add up to anything like an effective global response to challenges like climate change or unsustainable consumption. Some authors challenge this depiction of polycentrism as necessarily mired in the more general anarchy of international politics. Galaz and his colleagues, for example, argue that processes of information sharing, coordination of activities, problem-solving, and internal conflict resolution provide different degrees of "polycentric order" (Galaz et al. 2012; see also Dorsch and Flachsland 2017). Nevertheless, concerns about coordination, or orchestration (Abbott and Snidal 2010), motivate much of the literature on polycentric governance, especially in the context of climate change governance (e.g., Hale 2016), which Held and Hervey (2011) still characterize as suffering from "anarchic inefficiency." The first experiment in orchestration in polycentric climate governance is the Paris Agreement's portal, NAZCA (Non-State Actor Zone for Climate Action), which registers polycentric initiatives. The UNFCCC hopes that an annual dialogue will facilitate cooperation. Grounding such ideas in deliberative systems theory would strengthen their potential to deliver effective and legitimate outcomes.

A deliberative system can help make polycentrism work by enabling meaningful communication across disparate initiatives – and accountability of these initiatives to multilateral bodies to ensure collective goals can be met (as set out in Section 3.5).

An effective global deliberative system would productively join top-down and bottom-up approaches to governance. A crucial ingredient is the creation of platforms to gather and diffuse lessons learnt from local governance experiments, through networks such as the International Council for Local Environmental Initiatives (ICLEI). Linkages between local and multilateral efforts could be strengthened through processes of orchestration, where state and non-state organizations publicly commit to take action toward internationally agreed goals such as those in the Paris Agreement on climate change or the SDGs. A further linkage may occur when multilateral bodies periodically assess the functioning of polycentric systems (such as UN High-Level Panels on humanitarian financing, women's economic empowerment, and water).

An effective global deliberative system would also be capable of hosting deliberation on its own deliberative strengths and weaknesses – meta-deliberation. From the point of view of democratic legitimacy, meta-deliberation is essential if particular functions in a deliberative system are delegated to bodies such as expert assessments and networks that are not themselves intrinsically democratic (Landwehr 2015). We now examine how such meta-deliberation can facilitate the vital requirement for reflexivity in global institutions.

## 7 Reflexivity and Reconstruction

Deliberative global governance is a process for reconstruction as well as a set of institutions and practices, in that the steps taken toward reconfiguring of governance can and should themselves be inclusive and deliberative. The need for this kind of democratic meta-deliberation applies both to those rare occasions when comprehensive institutional innovation is on the agenda and to the more normal kind of situation when change can only be incremental. Reflexive institutions, structures, practices, and sets of ideas should be able to reconstruct themselves in light of reflection on their own performance.

## 7.1 Escaping Path Dependencies

Most institutional arrangements of any longevity are subject to path dependencies, which means they respond mostly to – and even create – feedback that reinforces their own necessity. Path dependency may be a good thing if institutional arrangements are producing manifestly good consequences (for example, when a regulatory agency keeps pollution under control). Path dependency becomes problematic or even pathological when it precludes responding to pressing and changing problems, such as potentially catastrophic developments in the Earth system (Dryzek and Pickering 2019: 22–23). Multilateral negotiations can absorb the political energies of national governments and civil society without producing any effective outcomes; for a long time the UNFCCC was like this. Banks and other financial institutions emerged from the 2008 global financial crisis very much as they were before, after being bailed out by governments in the interim.

Problematic path dependency can sometimes be escaped during what historical institutionalists call "critical junctures." In the international system, comprehensive innovation has occurred mostly in the aftermath of total war: in 1648, 1815, 1919, and 1945. The end of World War II yielded the United Nations and Bretton Woods systems for global economic governance – which still provide the basic institutional fabric for the international system. These institutional designs were negotiated through a mix of bargaining and deliberation, and heavily influenced by the United States as the dominant power.

If crisis or critical juncture does provide an opportunity for thoroughgoing institutional reconstruction, deliberation can be especially effective in yielding responses. Ackerman (1991) analyses three key episodes in US constitutional history – the founding in 1789, the Civil War, and the New Deal – to show that radical constitutional change was achieved through deliberative depth and breadth across all the existing institutions of government. The case of the New Deal suggests that a critical juncture can arise through economic crisis as well as war – though the Great Depression met with no effective *global* governance response. However, relying on crises or critical junctures to enable bursts of positive institutional change is risky because war, depression, and ecological collapse are exactly what institutions should be anticipating and avoiding – rather than welcoming as a catalyst for change.

In more ordinary times, institutional change is more like sailors rebuilding a ship while at sea than it is like shipbuilders constructing a vessel on land (Elster, Offe, and Preuss 1998). Thus, rather than wait for the kind of salvation that a critical juncture might (but might not) enable, it is important to cultivate a more thoroughgoing capacity for reconstruction. The opposite of the kind of pathological path dependency we have described is reflexivity: the capacity to reconfigure core institutional values, processes, and structures following reflection on their consequences. Reflexivity involves the ability to *be* something different rather than just *do* something different. In a world where dominant institutions are unfit for purpose, reflexivity becomes a core virtue for any institutional arrangements – deliberative or otherwise. Reflexivity enables thoroughgoing institutional change without rushing to prescription in a way that would short-circuit the learning that is necessary when facing novel and complex challenges. There are hints of reflexivity in how the European Union was gradually constructed over several decades. There can be moments along the way when institutional change accelerates, such as the establishment of the World Trade Organization in 1995 or the UNFCCC in 1992 (though as we have noted that was followed by 23 years of impasse).

## 7.2 Deliberative Sources of Reflexivity

Because reflection is at the heart of any meaningful deliberative process, such processes are especially good at yielding reflexivity (Dryzek and Pickering 2017). Making existing institutions more deliberative along the lines we described earlier is key to more thoroughgoing transformation. A deliberative perspective offers no blueprint that can or should be imposed on global governance. Rather, it is a way to think about how governance can be reconfigured.

This kind of deliberative learning in turn benefits from the inclusion of all those affected by an institution – or their representatives. A critical public sphere involving protest and civil society activism can help an institution break out of problematic path dependency. For example, the World Bank reflected upon and reconsidered some of its priorities, and its previous commitment to the neoliberalism of the Washington Consensus, in response to the antiglobalization movement beginning in 1999 (Stiglitz 2002).

Deliberation can also facilitate reflexive global governance by managing tensions between plausible proposals for how reflexivity should be cultivated. These tensions include those between polycentric and centralized governance, flexible and stable institutions, and diversity and consensus (Dryzek and Pickering 2017). Polycentrism's proponents believe it enables reflexivity by allowing for institutional experimentation in niches, which if successful can be more widely adopted; we have already described how a deliberative system can redeem polycentrism's promise.

Institutional flexibility is often seen as essential for reflexive governance, as it means that institutions can readily adapt to changing circumstances. However, without some degree of stability, institutions will fail to set in motion changes that are needed to address long-term problems, and they may be more vulnerable to capture by short-term interests. To address this tension, a global deliberative system could mix long-term goals for action on shared problems (set out for example in international treaties or declarations) with periodic review of the goals themselves as well as more frequent reviews of national contributions toward existing goals. Deliberative reviews would not be limited to assessing progress against goals that countries have set for themselves; crucially, these reviews would also challenge countries to raise the ambition of their contributions to global efforts. A balance between flexibility and stability could be struck by incorporating ratchet mechanisms to allow countries to lift their ambition but not backslide on their existing pledges. This kind of mechanism features in the Paris Agreement on climate change and could be adopted in other areas such as biodiversity conservation or protection of refugees.

A different kind of flexibility may be necessary to identify and respond to new global problems as they emerge. Some global institutions such as the UN Office for the Coordination of Humanitarian Affairs are designed (albeit imperfectly) to respond to unpredictable situations. But some emerging problems have no clear institutional counterparts at the global level, such as ocean plastic pollution or the online spread of misinformation. While durable global institutions may take years to materialize, an effective global deliberative system would help to transmit signs of emerging problems to decision-makers (e.g., through a global dissent channel and deliberative expert assessments) and generate ideas on how to resolve them (e.g., through the DGCA or nested forums).

Finally, deliberation can help resolve tensions between diversity and consensus within a global system. For some proponents of reflexive governance, "opening up" institutions to different perspectives is more important than "closing down" on specific policy options (see, e.g., Stirling 2008). A vibrant range of discourses and ideas is the lifeblood of a deliberative system, but ultimately the health of the system requires closure and action. Managing this tension proves especially important at the global level. In the words of the Brundtland Commission's pioneering report on sustainable development, "The Earth is one but the world is not" (WCED 1987). We have shown how global deliberation can come to terms with linguistic and cultural diversity, as well as highly varied forms of knowledge, experience, and values.

Rather than aiming at straightforward consensus on disputed issues, global diversity can be harnessed in *meta-consensus* (Dryzek and Niemeyer 2006). Meta-consensus involves seeking agreement on the legitimacy of contested values and beliefs, as well as the range of discourses that are acceptable in deliberation. To make progress on resolving disputes over territory, for example, it may be necessary to reach meta-consensus that a discourse proclaiming that one group's well-being or security is more important than that of the other has no place at the negotiating table. Resolving sectarian conflict may require meta-consensus on the legitimacy of each side's right to hold their own religious beliefs, but also constraints on employing religious arguments in negotiations that the other side may not accept.

Deliberative institutional reconfiguration in the service of reflexivity is realistic in that it tries to enlist actors already participating in global governance, be they states, international organizations, civil society activists, protestors, or public intellectuals. Everything we have said previously about the salutary effects of inclusive and authentic deliberation applies to processes of institutional reconstruction, which should be itself a matter for effective deliberation including all those affected.

We turn now to show how a deliberative approach can be applied in very practical terms to thinking about some of the major challenges confronting global governance in today's world.

## 8 Confronting Challenges

### 8.1 Climate Change

While the 2015 Paris Agreement suggested that the long impasse in the global response to climate change might finally show some signs of yielding, existing arrangements continue to fall short of what is required to prevent catastrophic climate change. Effective adaptation to the adverse consequences of climate change is faring little better. We show now how a deliberative approach could help produce more effective, ambitious, and accountable outcomes.

We have argued that engagement both in civil society (public space) and between civil society and decision-makers (empowered space) is necessary for effective deliberative global governance. A deliberative approach requires inclusive, meaningful, and consequential engagement across people who subscribe to different discourses. The deliberative system on climate change currently has shortcomings due to the symbolic or cosmetic inclusion of civil society in international forums and negotiations; gatherings of like-minded people in face-to-face and online enclaves who make no attempt to reach others; patterns of narrative accountability that place affected people in a position of passive audience; and an accountability vacuum in networked climate governance. We will outline specific proposals for remedying these shortcomings.

One sign of a healthy deliberative system is the presence of multiple discourses rather than discursive hegemony. Perhaps due to the complexity of the issue and the way in which it implicates social, economic, environmental, technological, and moral concerns, climate change attracts a great diversity of perspectives. Some reformist discourses stress the potential for low-carbon capitalism and the decoupling of greenhouse gas pollution and profit; others take a more expansive view of sustainability and see a decarbonizing capitalist economy as necessarily accompanied by greater public control and the transfer of technology from the North to the South. More radical discourses stress the planet's natural limits and the impossibility of endless economic growth in an ecologically finite world, the importance of re-localizing and downsizing production and consumption systems, or the need to dismantle structural inequalities that drive climate injustice.

The public sphere is not lacking in climate change discourses but does lack effective and inclusive engagement of discourses. There is a tendency toward discursive enclaves whereby reformists talk to other reformists, and radicals talk to other radicals. While many forums remain open in principle to participants of any discursive persuasion, they are framed and organized with a single discourse in mind. The selection of speakers projects this discourse, and the joint declarations that frequently accompany such events transmit this discourse to decision-makers and wider society. Stevenson and Dryzek (2014) observed this pattern of engagement in multiple civil society settings in the lead-up to the Copenhagen Climate Summit in 2009. A simple way to enhance the deliberative quality of climate change debates is for the business-oriented advocates of mainstream sustainability to encourage the participation of radical civil society, and vice versa. Encouraging those who think differently to speak is not enough; a commitment to listening to and understanding what others have to say is essential.

Tackling online enclaves is a greater challenge, and one far from unique to climate change debates. Social media enterprises could however develop "anti-echo chamber mechanisms" that alert the users of, say, Twitter to contrasting profiles. This is the opposite of existing mechanisms that encourage users to follow others like them. Unfortunately, the potential for such a mechanism to generate fruitful debate is undermined by the tendency for anonymous online communication to bring out the worst in people, as in climate change debates. In the United States, Canada, and Australia, a discourse of denialism has long dominated online forums in a way that far outweighs its presence in "real world" meetings. Denialist commentary is often offensive or personally insulting to climate scientists. The effect (and possibly the intent) is to undermine the conditions that would make fruitful deliberations on global climate governance possible. The kind of organized crowdsourcing we described in Section 4.4 could harness the benefits of large-scale online communication while avoiding the pitfalls of uncivil exchanges. Ideas about transitioning toward low-carbon societies are diverse and dispersed; no one group of experts has a monopoly on relevant knowledge. Hence, deliberative crowdsourcing has great potential in this context.

Much of global climate change governance occurs outside the UN system, and consequently often escapes the critical eye of civil society. The emergence of "polycentric" climate governance is in part a consequence of the slow pace of multilateral negotiations and the limited ambition of agreements which have left significant governance gaps. Some subnational and non-state actors have sought to fill these gaps by developing network governance arrangements of the kind we discussed in Section 3.5, involving private and provincial emission trading schemes, emissions offsetting schemes, efficiency targets, corporate reporting and information sharing, and voluntary targets and timetables for reducing greenhouse gas emissions. Governance gaps are not the only driver here. The dominant political-economic discourse of neoliberalism depicts the state as inefficient, which has led to regulatory retreat in much of the world, and places non-state actors in a strong position to set the parameters of their own mitigation strategies. The UN system itself is not well governed by democratic norms, but one advantage it has is that its visibility permits scrutiny, which can lead to accountability demands from inside and outside the United Nations. Encouraging civil society to broaden its focus and deploy limited resources to scrutinize rule-making bodies beyond the United Nations risks diluting the critical attention that already exists. Thinking about global governance in deliberative terms opens up new avenues for holding powerful actors and decision-makers to account. It allows us to rethink who is accountable to whom, for what, and why.

In a system where the decisions and actions of "global governors" can significantly impact human lives (including those of future generations), it is inadequate to think about accountability narrowly in principal-agent terms (negotiators to governments, or the UNFCCC secretariat to member states). Nor is it sufficient to think only in punitive terms. Accountability in the UNFCCC is largely understood in terms of compliance, that is, state compliance with pledges and promised action. Under the 1997 Kyoto Protocol this entailed reporting on progress toward reaching the unambitious targets and timetables negotiated for each industrialized member state. The emphasis on compliance shifted attention away from responsibility for the content of agreements. Justified as a "first step" in global climate governance, the collective target to reduce emissions by 5 percent below 1990 levels was completely out of step with the scale of the problem. Under the flexible rules of the 2015 Paris Agreement, each state determines the nature and ambition of its own targets and timetables. It is certainly debatable whether this largely "bottom-up" approach is more rigorous than "top-down" negotiated targets, but one potentially positive aspect is the demand for public justification that is built into self-determined target-setting. In submitting their climate change mitigation plans ("Nationally Determined Contributions" or NDCs), states have to justify the ambition of their pledges in light of both their domestic conditions and the demands of fair and equitable international burden-sharing. This style of justification reflects the narrative accountability described in Section 2.2 whereby actors explain and justify their decisions and actions to a wider audience. It imposes an expectation that the actor will consider the needs, interests, and perspectives of the audience who will ultimately judge, accept, or reject their account.

The transparency and compliance mechanisms of the Paris Agreement (Articles 13–15) have the potential to institutionalize deliberative accountability.

While there is no way to ensure that states increase their ambition over time, there is an expectation that they will do so. A stocktaking process is planned for 2023, and every subsequent five years, to review progress and ratchet up ambition. The mechanisms to support compliance and progressive ambition are non-punitive, non-judicial expert committees designed to understand countries' needs, circumstances, and progress toward achieving their commitments. The precise mandates of these committees are under negotiation and will likely evolve in the years ahead.

In the interim, Parties to the Paris Agreement decided to hold a facilitative dialogue throughout 2018 to assess collective progress and inform the next round of NDCs (UNFCCC 2015: paragraph 20). The "Talanoa Dialogue," as it has become known after Fiji's presidency of the UN climate conference in 2017, is inspired by the Polynesian tradition of *talanoa* ("a traditional approach used in Fiji and the Pacific to engage in an inclusive, participatory and transparent dialogue": UNFCCC 2017: Annex II). The structure and intent of the Dialogue reflect deliberative principles of openness, inclusion, equality, respect, sincerity, listening, and collective learning that draw on Western and non-Western traditions of deliberation. The preparatory phase of the Dialogue involves facilitated meetings in relatively small groups (each with representatives from about 30 states and 5 civil society organizations), guided by common questions of "Where are we?; Where do we want to go?; and How do we get there?" (Schrader 2018; UNFCCC 2017: Annex II). These meetings are supplemented by online inputs from states and civil society, and capped by a "political phase" in which high-level representatives bring together the results of the preceding discussions. The principles of the Dialogue could usefully be carried over to the longer-term Global Stocktake, but the challenge will remain to ensure that participants adhere to those principles rather than revert to inflexible negotiating stances.

This development offers a reason to be positive about the potential to integrate the transparency and compliance mechanisms of the Paris Agreement into a deliberative system that promotes deliberative orchestration and accountability, connects with civil society, and draws both the UNFCCC and polycentric governance initiatives into its purview.

Dialogue-based reviews could promote deliberative accountability by requiring both states and a diversely constituted review panel to ask questions and provide justifications in ways that promote reflection, learning, and attention to consequences. From a democratic perspective, there is great value in broadening participation in review panels beyond experts (just as seen in Section 3.6 regarding scientific assessments). Decision-making on most matters of public concern, including climate change, implicates elements of objective truth and falsity, as well as elements of judgment. The contribution of experts is important, but drawing on a broader "common wisdom" is also important for effective and legitimate outcomes. Consider the case of carbon capture and storage (CCS) technology. Review dialogues should take account of the $CO_2$ mitigation potential of CCS technologies. But they also must consider ethical arguments such as whether it is fair for industrialized countries to avoid domestic emissions reductions by investing in nascent technology in developing countries, or judgments about whether CCS projects are detracting from more "genuinely clean" renewable energy projects (UNFCCC 2014). By including civil society in review panels and drawing on their ethical and practical judgments about climate change mitigation and adaptation, the UNFCCC can deepen its connection with the global public sphere.

The 2015 Paris Agreement confirmed the importance of "hybrid multilateralism" and "orchestration" in global climate governance (Bäckstrand, Kuyper, Linnér, and Lövbrand 2017), joining top-down and bottom-up (polycentric) governance. Orchestration could enlist civil society intermediaries to monitor states' performance against national-level commitments. An orchestration body of state and civil society actors could also establish accountability chains between the UNFCCC, polycentric governance initiatives, and global civil society. The Non-State Actor Zone for Climate Action (NAZCA) is an online UN portal for cities, regions, businesses, and civil society to register their mitigation and adaptation initiatives. It is complemented by an annual dialogue between high-level officials (such as ministers) and non-state actors to assess voluntary progress (UNFCCC 2015: 17–18). These orchestration efforts could be integrated into the UNFCCC transparency and compliance committees. This integration would move us closer to a deliberative system to better ensure that actions within and beyond the UNFCCC work toward the goal of stabilizing the climate. This movement in turn would require increased investment of financial and human resources, as well as recognition by sub-state and non-state actors that there are legitimacy gains to be achieved from signing up to systemic oversight.

## 8.2 Peacebuilding

As a seemingly civil form of communication, deliberation may appear to be most suited to durably peaceful societies, while deep conflicts require instead elite agreement and coercive external supervision (Call and Cook 2003: 233). Not so. Deliberative democracy can apply to deep conflicts based on ethnicity, nationality, or religion (O'Flynn 2017). This application can involve leaders from different sides agreeing to share power, but that is only part of the story.

Deliberation in informal "track II" diplomacy involving non-state actors from different sides can generate good ideas for the shape of a resolution. Former combatants can deliberate with each other – in Colombia, leftist guerillas and right-wing paramilitaries (Steiner, Jaramillo, Maia, and Mameli 2017). Productive engagements can involve lay citizens as well as leaders, focusing on practical matters (for example, education, policing, security) rather than the high politics of power claims. While most successful examples of deliberative conflict resolution currently come from within state boundaries rather than across them, that is in keeping with the nature of contemporary violent conflict. Overt war between states is now rare (Clauset 2018). More common are civil conflicts – which may however be sponsored by outside states, and sometimes spill over borders.

The basic premise of peacebuilding is that peace is not necessarily sustainable just because a conflict has paused and a state has managed to secure some authority (Andrieu 2010). Lasting peace requires mutual understanding and some form of reconciliation between conflicting groups. Otherwise, enmities fester, inherited by subsequent generations, locking in the prospect of future conflicts. The peacebuilding outlook is now "firmly established on the international security agenda" (Barnett 2006: 87). There are many affinities between deliberative democracy and peacebuilding, which seeks to reconstruct relationships in post-conflict societies according to norms of trust, respect, and equity. Dialogue can then work with society-specific traditions – for example, what Braithwaite and Gohar (2014) call "Eastern deliberative democracy" in discussing cases that provide an alternative to both Taliban brutality and cycles of revenge in providing local justice in Pakistan. Peacebuilding is democratic to the degree it involves society-wide dialogue, and publics drawn from different sides in a search for mutual understanding and reconciliation.

Peacebuilding depends upon engagement between conflicting groups and with their victims. A key feature of such processes is the notion of transitional justice which involves "processes and mechanisms associated with a society's attempts to come to terms with a legacy of large-scale past abuses, in order to ensure accountability, serve justice and achieve reconciliation. These may include ... individual prosecutions, reparations, truth-seeking, institutional reform, vetting and dismissals, or a combination thereof" (UN 2004). Such undertakings often aim to establish the truth of what happened. Equally important is the opportunity for victims to express their experiences and to be recognized by perpetrators and a wider audience (Mendeloff 2004: 359). Ideally, victims and perpetrators create a new shared self-understanding, one that recognizes the past, but also puts the past to rest, allowing a new forward-looking orientation to emerge. Where these dimensions of peace have been ignored in top-down programs, peacebuilding has met with little success (Lederach 1997). Barnett (2006) suggests that if international leaders attended to the history of their own nations, they would appreciate that reconciliation and acceptance can take decades to secure. This challenge involves not only building robust state institutions but also establishing a deliberative culture with respect to the past. Such a culture presupposes that parties are motivated to engage each other respectfully and able to see events from the other side. Even where such encounters do not yield forgiveness, the mere fact of being prepared to sustain the encounter connotes progress (Andrieu 2010).

Bohman (2012) suggests that peace achieved in Northern Ireland embodies a multilevel and multistage deliberative process. Civil society connections between Unionists and Republicans grew independently of the negotiations and associated relationships between leaders. These ground-level relationships allowed peace to be built from the bottom-up, forming a "peace constituency" that lessened the centrality of elite bargaining to the peace process. However, what elites do remains important in deliberative terms, not just in their negotiations, but also in their public framing of issues. Leaders can sometimes choose bridging rhetoric that reaches across historical divides – consider Nelson Mandela's appeals to white South Africans in the transition from apartheid, which facilitated productive exchanges. Unfortunately, leaders can choose to do exactly the opposite: consider Serbian President Slobodan Milosevic's inflammatory appeals to Serb identity as Yugoslavia fell apart in the 1990s.

Injustices inflicted in war are difficult to resolve legally due to the compromised state of legal institutions, either wrecked by war or used by one side. In such settings, hybrid deliberative practices can often be put to good use (Braithwaite 2015). Hybrid here refers to the fusion of formal legal processes with elements of traditional culture, which often involve considerable amounts of carefully structured deliberation. Wardak and Braithwaite (2013) show how deliberative processes at the village level have reduced crime and conflict in Afghanistan. Restorative justice practices, which have an affinity with deliberative democracy (Parkinson and Roche 2004), have been used to put an end to deadly blood feuds. These processes enable reconciliation between people who must live in close proximity but who have committed atrocities against one another (Wardak and Braithwaite 2013: 203). Such practices fall short of due process standards entrenched in Western legal systems, but they are justifiable given that formal legal systems are unlikely to be consolidated in the near term. Some justice is better than none, especially when it lessens the likelihood of more conflict.

Mendeloff (2004) argues that there remains an enormous amount to be understood about organized truth-telling, a central pillar of peacebuilding and equally central to deliberative democracy. The mechanisms through which post-conflict truth-telling generates desirable social and psychological consequences have been little studied, and it is conceivable that truth-telling may sometimes inflame conflict. Braithwaite and Nickson (2012) examine truth and reconciliation commissions (now seen as integral to peace-building) and how their timing affects the likelihood of lasting peace. South Africa's Truth and Reconciliation Commission demonstrated the potential of deliberative reconciliation across deep difference. However, in post-conflict situations, the international community is often eager to secure "peace" then quickly withdraw, meaning a rush to institute commissions too soon. This fails to allow that those most traumatized by a conflict, or those most deeply complicit, may take a long time to engage with such processes. In the case of military atrocities, senior military figures are more likely to engage once, for example, collective confessions have been made by military units. More generally, participation in such truth-telling processes is only likely at all when potential participants have confidence that providing details of their crimes will not result in revenge attacks or retribution. The successful democratic transition in Spain, for example, featured negotiated silence surrounding the atrocities that occurred under Franco's dictatorship (Encarnación 2014). In this light, Braithwaite and Nickson (2012) propose that truth and reconciliation commissions should often be seen as more permanent institutions. The point here is not to pour cold water on deliberative peacebuilding, but rather to underscore that in any complex setting, deliberative democracy should be thought of as a process of reflexivity and reconstruction (see Section 7), not the imposition of a model. Conflict and its resolution involve complex social, political, and psychological process and are not amenable to simple fixes. Public deliberation is central in bringing about the reconciliation upon which peace depends.

## 8.3 Confronting Poverty: Deliberative Global Justice

For several decades, the dominant conception of justice in the global system has been a neoliberal one that emphasizes free market-based exchange and private property rights. This conception is dominant because it is embedded in regimes and institutions that are themselves dominant – such as the global trade and finance regimes, and organizations such as the IMF and the WTO. While neoliberalism is not supported by most people who think they are advocating justice, it fulfils the formal requirements of a theory of justice as a full account of the proper distribution of benefits and burdens in the global system. When redistribution does overcome neoliberal opposition to reach the global agenda, it has often been seen as a matter of international justice – the units of both obligation and concern are states, not people. For example, questions of climate justice were long debated in terms of the relative obligations and claims that different kinds of states (rich and poor) should have. The necessity to move beyond such limited ideas is now widely recognized. For example, the Millennium Development Goals (MDGs) adopted by the United Nations in 2000 owed much to the idea that justice should be sought in human development – health, education, gender equality, and poverty eradication – not just in redistribution of resources between countries. But how should global justice move forward?

The idea that this movement should be made in deliberative and participatory fashion is gaining some currency. The MDGs were formulated by a small group of UN experts, with no deliberative or participatory aspect to their formulation or implementation. Recognizing these limitations, the process that in 2015 yielded the successor Sustainable Development Goals (SDGs) involved a vast number of forums and consultations. There remained substantial deliberative shortcomings, especially in the highly skewed access to consultations – corporations and NGOs based in wealthy countries had much more input than those in developing countries. But some deliberative features were on display, for example in the Open Working Group that finalized the content of the SDGs and their associated targets. The Open Working Group had 30 seats, each of which was shared by three countries; the three often came from different blocs (e.g., Nepal, Iran, and Japan) so they had to generate common positions that often cut across bloc divisions. Face-to-face deliberation is possible with 30 participants; it is unwieldy with 193 (the number of countries that adopted the SDGs).

Shortcomings notwithstanding, the participatory intentions of the SDG process suggest there is a demand for inclusive deliberation in advancing the global antipoverty agenda – and in expanding that agenda into related areas of development. But why exactly is deliberative democracy a good idea in goal-setting and other efforts to advance global justice?

Deliberation is necessary to determine exactly what justice requires, both generally in exercises such as the SDGs and in specific development contexts. Assuming there is a common desire to alleviate poverty, how best should it be approached? Should the essence be monetary transfers from the rich to the poor, or greater fairness in trade relations? If it is money, should transfers be made to governments in developing countries to administer, or should the vulnerability of these governments to corruption or mismanagement mean they should be bypassed by engaging NGOs on the ground? On what should expenditures be targeted – combating diseases, or providing safe drinking water, or better housing? It is possible for experts to calculate the most cost-effective expenditures in terms of lives saved per thousand dollars spent (as recommended by the "effective altruism" movement), but no metric is neutral. When it comes to lives saved, do children matter more? Do aid expenditures undermine the political capacity of marginalized communities to organize? Someone needs to deliberate these questions – and not just experts, or those with money to distribute.

Deliberation is required not only on what actions justice requires but also on what justice *means* to begin with. Is justice a matter of alleviating the suffering of the most disadvantaged, fairness in income distribution, human rights, recognition of the full social and political standing of the marginalized, protection of private property, or promoting the development of human capabilities? To what extent should the traditional "international" way of thinking about justice as a matter of the relations between states (as in the notion of "common but differentiated responsibilities" of rich and poor countries for combatting climate change) give way to a concern for (and obligations of) people irrespective of which states they happen to live in? Does justice involve obligations to future generations, as well as within the present generation? Given reasonable disagreement about what justice means, and so what should be done in any given context, the only defensible solution is democratic deliberation that involves all those affected by such determinations, or their representatives (Sen 2009; Dryzek 2013).

The mere language of justice is not enough here. In global politics, many actors are adept at veiling their material self-interest in the language of justice, in, for example, multilateral negotiations. Sometimes appeals to material self-interest are defensible: residents of low-lying parts of Bangladesh have a material interest in not being drowned as a result of climate change, and that is also a matter of justice. But justice claims can be used in objectionably strategic ways too (see the discussion of multilateral negotiations in Section 3.1). For example, in negotiations over the SDGs, Saudi Arabia wanted energy to be included as a need of the poor, and as necessary for the economic growth needed to lift people out of poverty (Kamau, Chasek, and O'Connor 2018: 84 and 114). Goal 7 on affordable and clean energy reflects this position and says nothing about the harm caused by fossil fuels, still less about the need to transition to renewable energy to combat climate change – the Saudi negotiators opposed any linkage here. Climate change was addressed elsewhere in the SDGs (under Goal 13 on climate action), but what happened over Goal 7 appears to be a deliberative failure. For despite their interdependence, energy access and climate change were not deliberated together. Instead, they were simply assigned different places in an ever-expanding list of goals and targets.

If actors think justice is on their side, they may become more intransigent in global negotiations: this applies to the G77 bloc of developing countries as much as it does the United States, which advance very different ideas about climate justice (and other issues). For the G77, climate justice is historical in that countries which have built their prosperity on a long history of fossil fuel use should bear the major burden of emissions reduction. For the US, climate justice means fairness in the terms of trade, which would be violated if wealthier countries must bear costs of emissions reduction which their less industrialized competitors avoid. This potential intransigence is an additional reason why justice claims need to be deliberated – not just asserted – to determine whether they withstand scrutiny, or are merely a rationalization of self-interest.

One major problem arises in contemplating the disproportionate role exercised by wealthy actors in defining global justice – especially when it comes to poverty alleviation. By definition, the wealthy are people and organizations who have resources that could be redistributed. Now, redistribution could be organized by some public authority that levies taxes and decides where the money should go. Or it could be – and sometimes is – organized by the rich themselves, possibly acting on advice from public intellectuals such as Sachs (2005) and Singer (2009), who advocate global redistribution. Sometimes it is individual donors who respond to the call to give money. Sometimes it is very large private foundations. The Gates Foundation disburses around $4 billion a year, making it a dominant player in health and agriculture, buying it a place in global policy-making.

The problem with letting wealthy actors decide for themselves how money should be spent is that it constructs a political hierarchy in which the poor are subject to the discretionary choices of the rich. Republican thinkers such as Pettit (1997) insist that the essence of freedom is *not* being subject to the discretionary choices of others – be they wealthy donors, foundations, or international organizations.

As Kuper (2002: 116) puts it, this approach to poverty alleviation sees the poor as "moral patients" dependent on the goodwill of donors rather than political agents capable of determining their own future. This hierarchy means that information crucial for effective decision-making is lost: the lived experience of the poor themselves, what poverty really means to the people who endure it. Poverty may mean a lack of the basic needs of life; it may also mean income insecurity, feelings of vulnerability and disempowerment, or being at the mercy of others. This information is essential to determining what should be done, involving not just how money should be spent (be it on drilling wells for clean water or mosquito nets to restrict malaria) but potentially also political empowerment, the ability to self-organize, full social and legal recognition, and structural change to enable more effective economic participation.

The need for direct participation to resolve these sorts of questions has two deliberative implications. The first has been put forward by Amartya Sen (2009), for whom the active participation of the poor in controlling their own lives is essential to justice. At a local level, evidence suggests that the poor and marginalized can be effective deliberators in helping determine the content of justice. Rao and Sanyal (2010: 254) show how deliberation in *gram sabhas* (state-mandated village assemblies) in South India can involve the participation of low-caste individuals in a way that "creates a relatively level discursive field." "Deliberation shapes the meaning of poverty" and what to do about it, with consequences for the allocation of expenditures (Rao and Sanyal 2010: 164–167).

The second implication is more demanding: it requires the participation of the poor in global processes that determine what poverty alleviation and global justice should mean, from which they are almost always missing (though a few attempts were made in specific localities in the formulation of the SDGs). This can be done by the poor themselves organizing to act globally. La Via Campesina, the global peasants and small farmers movement, is organized from the grassroots up into an international federation. In addition, institutional design could enable direct participation. Earlier we discussed a deliberative global citizens' assembly and other kinds of mini-publics and forums. These could be constituted in ways that involve targeted recruitment of the poor and marginalized. Limited experience at the global level includes the Participate Initiative, which organized "ground level panels" to promote the voices of the marginalized in the process that yielded the Sustainable Development Goals (Howard and Wheeler 2015).

In the absence of the poor themselves participating in global processes, what happens is that activists and advocacy groups such as CARE International or Save the Children step in. They can have a problematic relationship with those they claim to represent, for example when celebrity activists in the "Make Poverty History" campaign depicted the poor as helpless subordinate claimants on the charity of the rich (highlighted by an African reaction of "Not About Us Without Us"). These problems can to a degree be alleviated by more effective communication between advocates and the poor – and by efforts by advocates to raise the political capacities of the poor so they are better able to participate (Montanaro 2018). Advocates could work to develop accountability bonds with the poor (rather than substituting for the poor in global processes). Once this relationship is in good order, claims can be made more effectively and legitimately to global governance processes involving states and international organizations, such as the High-Level Forum on Sustainable Development.

Currently, the dominant actors that determine what poverty and justice should mean and what should be done in response are international organizations, states, foundations, and other wealthy donors. Next come service-delivery NGOs (the world's biggest is Bangladesh's BRAC), advocacy groups and public intellectuals (such as Sachs and Singer). Last of all come lay citizens and the poor themselves. As we have indicated, all these actors have their problems or challenges, ranging from the tendency of states to interpret justice in self-interested fashion, to the wealthy establishing relations of charity that yield political hierarchies, to advocates who construct the poor in demeaning ways, to the lack of deliberative opportunity for the poor. These actors all need integrating into a global deliberative system. The elements of this integration should include more direct participation by the poor and vulnerable, improved communication and accountability between advocates and the poor they claim to represent, and the embedding of foundations, states, and international organizations in relationships that mean they must justify and be prepared to change the positions they take in ways that respond to more than just their own interests or perceptions. An inclusive deliberative system would mean that global justice gets defined and pursued in ways that are responsive to the real needs and concerns of those who need it most.

## 9 Conclusion

We have argued that deliberative democratization can yield more legitimate and effective global governance, and contribute to a more sustainable, peaceful, and just world. Deliberation is well suited to the global level, where, due to the absence of state-like sovereign authority, persuasion is critical. Deliberative processes typically prioritize common interests and public goods. They also represent the most productive way of reconciling differences about what the common good entails (and of overcoming many other kinds of division as well). Deliberative democracy can therefore serve the good of all humankind. It is a deeply democratic approach, premised on the equal value of all human beings.

Deliberative governance is realistic in recognizing how power can pervade political communication – and in generating ways to counteract dominant discourses that serve some interests and repress others. Deliberative governance is feasible because it is grounded in the cultural universality of deliberation, while allowing variety in how the capacity for deliberation is exercised.

Above all, deliberative democracy is a creative and transformative project that can enlist global publics in the search for a more democratic, peaceful, just, and sustainable world. Effective deliberative systems can reconfigure core values, processes, and structures following reflection on their own performance. Institutional change can never be the adoption of someone's model – or even the outcome of a competition between models. While we have outlined some ideas for the shape we think deliberative global governance ought to take, we accept that a deliberative and democratic process of reconstruction might yield very different – and possibly better – results.

# References

Abbott, Kenneth W. and Duncan Snidal. 2010. International Regulation without International Government: Improving IO Performance through Orchestration. *Review of International Organizations* 5: 315–344.

Ackerman, Bruce A. 1991. *We the People I: Foundations.* Cambridge, MA: Harvard University Press.

Aitamurto, Tanja and Hélène Landemore. 2016. Crowdsourced Deliberation: The Case of the Law on Off-Road Traffic in Finland. *Policy and Internet* 8 (2): 174–196.

Allison, Graham T. 1971. *Essence of Decision: Explaining the Cuban Missile Crisis.* Boston, MA: Little Brown.

Alter, Karen J. and Sophie Meunier. 2009. The Politics of International Regime Complexity. *Perspectives on Politics* 7 (1): 13–24.

Andrieu, Kora. 2010. Civilizing Peacebuilding: Transitional Justice, Civil Society, and the Liberal Paradigm. *Security Dialogue* 41 (5): 537–558.

Avant, Deborah, Martha Finnemore, and Susan K. Sell. 2010. Who Governs the Global? In *Who Governs the Globe?*, ed. Deborah Avant, Martha Finnemore, and Susan K. Sell, pp. 1–31. Cambridge: Cambridge University Press.

Baber, Walter F. and Robert V. Bartlett. 2015. *Consensus and Global Environmental Governance: Deliberative Democracy in Nature's Regime.* Cambridge, MA: MIT Press.

Bäckstrand, Karin, Jonathan W. Kuyper, Björn-Ola Linnér, and Eva Lövbrand. 2017. Non-State Actors in Global Climate Governance: From Copenhagen to Paris and Beyond. *Environmental Politics* 26 (6): 561–579.

Barnett, Michael. 2006. Building a Republican Peace: Stabilizing States after War. *International Security* 30 (4): 87–112.

Barvosa, Edwina. 2018. *Deliberative Democracy Now: LGBT Equality and the Emergence of Large-Scale Deliberative Systems.* Cambridge: Cambridge University Press.

Beck, Silke, Maud Borie, Jason Chilvers, Alejandro Esguerra, Katja Heubach, Mike Hulme, Rolf Lidskog, Eva Lövbrand, Elisabeth Marquard, Clark Miller, Tahani Nadim, Carsten Neßhöver, Josef Settele, Esther Turnhout, Eleftheria Vasileiadou, and Christoph Görg. 2014. Towards a Reflexive Turn in the Governance of Global Environmental Expertise: The Cases of the IPCC and the IPBES. *GAIA – Ecological Perspectives for Science and Society* 23 (2): 80–87.

Benhabib, Seyla. 1996. Toward a Deliberative Model of Democratic Legitimacy. In *Democracy and Difference: Contesting the Boundaries of the Political*, ed. Seyla Benhabib, pp. 67–94. Princeton, NJ: Princeton University Press.

Berman, Paul Schiff. 2006. Global Legal Pluralism. *Southern California Law Review* 80: 1155–1237.

Bevir, Mark and Quinlan Bowman. 2011. Innovations in Democratic Governance. In *Innovations in Public Governance*, ed. Ari-Veikko Anttiroiko, Stephen J. Bailey, and Pekka Valkama, pp. 174–193. Amsterdam: IOS Press.

Bienkov, Adam. 2012. Astroturfing: What Is It and Why Does It Matter? The Guardian. February 9.

Birnbaum, Simon, Örjan Bodin, and Annica Sandström. 2015. Tracing the Sources of Legitimacy: The Impact of Deliberation in Participatory Natural Resource Management. *Policy Sciences* 48 (4): 443–461.

Bohman, James. 2012. Jus post bellum as a Deliberative Process: Transnationalising Peace-Building. *Irish Journal of Sociology* 20(2): 10–27.

Braithwaite, John. 2015. Deliberative Republican Hybridity through Restorative Justice. *Raisons Politques* 3 (59): 39–45.

Braithwaite, John and Ali Gohar. 2014. Restorative Justice, Policing and Insurgency: Learning from Pakistan. *Law and Society Review* 48 (3): 531–561.

Braithwaite, John and Ray Nickson. 2012. Timing Truth, Reconciliation, and Justice after War. *Ohio State Journal of Dispute Resolution* 27 (3): 443–476.

Buchanan, Allen. 2004. *Justice, Legitimacy, and Self-Determination*. Oxford: Oxford University Press.

Cabrera, Luis. 2004. *Political Theory of Global Justice: A Cosmopolitan Case for the World State*. London: Routledge.

Call, Charles T. and Susan E. Cook. 2003. On Democratization and Peacebuilding. *Global Governance* 9: 233–246.

Chambers, Simone. 2004. Behind Closed Doors: Publicity, Secrecy, and the Quality of Deliberation. *Journal of Political Philosophy* 12 (4): 389–410.

Chambers, Simone and Jeffrey Kopstein. 2001. Bad Civil Society. *Political Theory* 29 (6): 837–865.

Chasek, Pamela S, Lynn M. Wagner, Faye Leone, Anna-Maria Lebada, and Natalie Risse. 2016. Getting to 2030: Negotiating the Post-2015 Sustainable Development Agenda. *Review of European, Comparative and International Law* 25 (1): 5–14.

Clauset, Aaron. 2018. Trends and Fluctuations in the Severity of Interstate Wars. *Science Advances* 4 (2): 1–9.

Coleman, Stephen and Giles Moss. 2012. Under Construction: The Field of Online Deliberation Research. *Journal of Information Technology and Politics* 9: 1–15.

Crosby, Ted and Doug Nethercut. 2005. Citizens Juries: Creating a Trustworthy Voice of the People. In *The Deliberative Democracy Handbook: Strategies for Effective Citizen Engagement in the 21st Century*, ed. John Gastil and Peter Levine, pp. 111–119. San Francisco, CA: Jossey-Bass.

Curato, Nicole, Marit Hammond, and John Min. 2019. *Power in Deliberative Democracy: Norms, Forums, Systems*. Basingstoke: Palgrave Macmillan.

Dingwerth, Klaus, Henning Schmidtke, Tobias Weise, and Jonas Wodarz. 2015. Speaking Democracy: Why International Organizations Adopt a Democratic Rhetoric. Paper presented at ECPR Joint Sessions, Warsaw.

Dorsch, Marcel and Christian Flachsland. 2017. A Polycentric Approach to Global Climate Governance. *Global Environmental Politics* 17 (2): 45–64.

Drezner, Daniel W. 2009. The Power and Peril of International Regime Complexity. *Perspectives on Politics* 7 (1): 65–70.

Dryzek, John S. 2006. *Deliberative Global Politics: Discourse and Democracy in a Divided World*. Cambridge: Polity Press.

Dryzek, John S. 2010. *Foundations and Frontiers of Deliberative Governance*. Oxford: Oxford University Press.

Dryzek, John S. 2012. Global Civil Society: The Progress of Post-Westphalian Politics. *Annual Review of Political Science* 15: 101–119.

Dryzek, John S. 2013. The Deliberative Democrat's Idea of Justice. *European Journal of Political Theory* 12: 329–346.

Dryzek, John S., André Bächtiger, and Karolina Milewicz. 2011. Toward a Deliberative Global Citizens' Assembly. *Global Policy* 2: 33–42.

Dryzek, John S. and Simon Niemeyer. 2006. Reconciling Pluralism and Consensus as Political Ideals. *American Journal of Political Science* 50 (3): 634–649.

Dryzek, John S. and Jonathan Pickering. 2017. Deliberation as a Catalyst for Reflexive Environmental Governance. *Ecological Economics* 131: 353–360.

Dryzek, John S. and Jonathan Pickering. 2019. *The Politics of the Anthropocene*. Oxford: Oxford University Press.

Elster, Jon. 1998. Deliberation and Constitution Making. In *Deliberative Democracy*, ed. Jon Elster, pp. 97–122. Cambridge: Cambridge University Press.

Elster, Jon, Claus Offe, and Ulrich K. Preuss. 1998. *Institutional Design in Post-Communist Countries: Rebuilding the Ship at Sea*. Cambridge: Cambridge University Press.

Encarnación, Omar G. 2014. *Democracy without Justice in Spain: The Politics of Forgetting*. Philadelphia, PA: University of Pennsylvania Press.

Esaiasson, Peter, Mikael Gilljam, and Mikael Persson. 2017. Responsiveness Beyond Policy Satisfaction: Does It Matter to Citizens? *Comparative Political Studies* 50 (6): 739–765.

Evans, Peter and Martha Finnemore. 2001. Organizational Reform and the Expansion of the South's Voice at the Fund. G-24 Discussion Paper Series, No.15, Harvard University.

Falk, Richard and Andrew Strauss, eds. 2011. *A Global Parliament: Essays and Articles*. Berlin: Committee for a Democratic U.N.

Finnemore, Martha and Kathryn Sikkink. 1998. International Norm Dynamics and Political Change. *International Organization* 52 (4): 887–917.

Fishkin, James. 1995. *The Voice of the People: Public Opinion and Democracy*. New Haven, CT: Yale University Press.

Fishkin, James. 2009. *When the People Speak: Deliberative Democracy and Public Consultation*. Oxford: Oxford University Press.

Fishkin, James. 2018. *Democracy When the People are Thinking: Revitalizing our Politics through Public Deliberation*. Oxford: Oxford University Press.

Forstater, Maya. 2015. Can Stopping 'Tax Dodging' by Multinational Enterprises Close the Gap in Development Finance? Washington, DC: Center for Global Development, Policy Paper 69.

Franks, Max, Kai Lessmann, Michael Jakob, Jan Christoph Steckel, and Ottmar Edenhofer. 2018. Mobilizing Domestic Resources for the Agenda 2030 via Carbon Pricing. *Nature Sustainability* 1 (7): 350–357.

Galaz, Victor, Beatrice Crobna, Henrik Österblom, Per Olsson, and Carl Folke. 2012. Polycentric Systems and Interacting Planetary Boundaries. *Ecological Economics* 81: 21–32.

Gellers, Joshua C. 2016. Crowdsourcing Global Governance: Sustainable Development Goals, Civil Society, and the Pursuit of Democratic Legitimacy. *International Environmental Agreements: Politics, Law and Economics* 16 (3): 415–432.

Gettleman, Jeffrey. 2017. State Dept. Dissent Cable on Trump's Ban Draws 1,000 Signatures. New York Times, 31 January. www.nytimes.com/2017/01/31/world/americas/state-dept-dissent-cable-trump-immigration-order.html accessed 3 June 2019.

Gilabert, Pablo and Holly Lawford-Smith. 2012. Political Feasibility: A Conceptual Exploration. *Political Studies* 60 (4): 809–825.

Goodin, Robert E. 2010. Global Democracy: In the Beginning. *International Theory* 2 (2): 175–209.

Grant, Ruth W. and Robert O. Keohane. 2005. Accountability and Abuses of Power in World Politics. *American Political Science Review* 99 (1): 29–43.

Grönlund, Kimmo, André Bächtiger, and Maija Setälä, eds. 2014. *Deliberative Mini-Publics: Involving Citizens in the Democratic Process.* Colchester: ECPR Press.

Gurman, Hannah. 2011. The Other Plumbers Unit: The Dissent Channel of the U.S. State Department. *Diplomatic History* 35 (2): 321–349.

Gutmann, Amy and Dennis Thompson. 2004. *Why Deliberative Democracy?* Princeton, NJ: Princeton University Press.

Haas, Peter M. 1992. Banning Chlorofluorocarbons: Epistemic Community Efforts to Protect Stratospheric Ozone. *International Organization* 46 (1): 187–224.

Hale, Thomas. 2016. "All Hands on Deck": The Paris Agreement and Nonstate Climate Action. *Global Environmental Politics* 16 (3): 12–22.

Hardt, Michael and Antonio Negri. 2001. *Empire.* Cambridge, MA: Harvard University Press.

Harris, Paul G. 2011. Reconceptualizing Global Governance. In *The Oxford Handbook of Climate Change and Society*, ed. John S. Dryzek, Richard B. Norgaard, and David Schlosberg, pp. 639–652. Oxford: Oxford University Press.

Hartz-Karp, Janette, Patrick Anderson, John Gastil, and Andrea Felicetti. 2010. The Australian Citizens' Parliament: Forging Shared Identity through Public Deliberation. *Journal of Public Affairs* 10 (4): 353–71.

Hébert, Martin. 2018. Indigenous Spheres of Deliberation. In *The Oxford Handbook of Deliberative Democracy*, ed. André Bächtiger, John S. Dryzek, Jane Mansbridge, and Mark E. Warren, pp. 100–111. Oxford: Oxford University Press.

Held, David and Angus Fane-Hervey. 2011. Democracy, Climate Change, and Global Governance: Democratic Agency and the Policy Menu Ahead. In *The Governance of Climate Change: Science, Politics and Ethics*, ed. David Held, Marika Theros, and Angus Fane-Hervey, pp. 89–110. Cambridge: Polity.

Hendriks, Carolyn M. 2008. On Inclusion and Network Governance: The Democratic Disconnect of Dutch Energy Transitions. *Public Administration* 86 (4): 1009–31.

Henrich, Joseph, Robert Boyd, Samuel Bowles, Colin Camerer, Ernst Fehr, and Herbert Gintis. 2004. *Foundations of Human Sociality: Economic Experiments and Ethnographic Evidence from Fifteen Small-Scale Societies.* Oxford: Oxford University Press.

Higgott, Richard and Eva Erman. 2010. Deliberative Global Governance and the Question of Legitimacy: What Can we learn from the WTO? *Review of International Studies* 36: 449–470.

Hoffmann, Matthew J. 2011. *Climate Governance at the Crossroads: Experimenting with a Global Response after Kyoto.* Oxford: Oxford University Press.

Hopmann, P. Terrence. 1995. Two Paradigms of Negotiation: Bargaining and Problem Solving. *ANNALS of the American Academy of Political and Social Science* 542 (1): 24–47.

Howard, Jo and Joanna Wheeler. 2015. What Community Development and Citizen Participation Should Contribute to the New Global Framework for Sustainable Development. *Community Development Journal* 50 (4): 552–570.

Huntington, Samuel P. 1996. *The Clash of Civilizations and the Remaking of World Order.* New York: Simon and Schuster.

IEO (Independent Evaluation Office). 2011. IMF Performance in the Run-Up to the Financial and Economic Crisis: IMF Surveillance in 2004–2007. www .ieo-imf.org/ieo/files/completedevaluations/crisis-%20main%20report%20 (without%20moises%20signature).pdf accessed 12 July 2018.

Ikenberry, G. John. 2009. *After Victory: Institutions, Strategic Restraint, and the Rebuilding of Order after Major Wars.* Princeton: Princeton University Press.

Internet World Stats. 2018. www.internetworldstats.com/stats.htm accessed 13 July 2018.

Jacob Neusner and Bruce Chilton, eds. 2009. *The Golden Rule: The Ethics of Reciprocity in World Religions.* London: Continuum.

Kahneman, Daniel. 2011. *Thinking, Fast and Slow.* New York: Farrar, Straus and Giroux.

Kahneman, Daniel. 2018. Daniel Kahneman on Misery, Memory, And Our Understanding Of The Mind. www.npr.org/templates/transcript/transcript .php?storyId=592986190&t=1552733303316 accessed 15 March 2019.

Kaldor, Mary. 2003. The Idea of Global Civil Society. *International Affairs* 79: 583–593.

Kamau, Macharia, Pamela Chasek, and David O'Connor. 2018. *Transforming Multilateral Diplomacy: The Inside Story of the Sustainable Development Goals.* London: Routledge.

Keohane, Robert O. 2015. Nominal Democracy? Prospects for Democratic Global Governance. *International Journal of Constitutional Law* 13 (2): 343–353.

Keohane. Robert O., and Joseph S. Nye. 1977. *Power and Interdependence: World Politics in Transition.* Boston: Little Brown.

Keohane, Robert O. and David G. Victor. 2011. The Regime Complex for Climate Change. *Perspectives on Politics* 9 (1): 7–23.

Krasner, Stephen D. 1983. *International Regimes.* Ithaca, NY: Cornell University Press.

Krisch, Nico. 2010. *Beyond Constitutionalism: The Pluralist Structure of Postnational Law*. New York: Oxford University Press.

Kuper, Andrew. 2002. More than Charity: Cosmopolitan Alternatives to the "Singer Solution." *Ethics and International Affairs* 16: 107–120.

Kuyper, Jonathan W. 2014. Global Democratization and International Regime Complexity. *European Journal of International Relations* 20 (3): 620–646.

Kuyper, Jonathan W. and John S. Dryzek. 2016. Real, Not Nominal, Global Democracy: A Reply to Robert Keohane. *International Journal of Constitutional Law* 14 (4): 930–937.

Kuziemko, Ilyana and Eric Werker. 2006. How Much Is a Seat on the Security Council Worth? Foreign Aid and Bribery at the United Nations. *Journal of Political Economy* 114 (5): 905–930.

Landemore, Hélène. 2013. *Democratic Reason: Politics, Collective Intelligence, and the Rule of the Many*. Princeton, NJ: Princeton University Press.

Landemore, Hélène. 2015. Inclusive Constitution-Making: The Icelandic Experiment. *Journal of Political Philosophy* 23 (2): 166–191.

Landwehr, Claudia. 2015. Democratic Meta-Deliberation: Towards Reflective Institutional Design. *Political Studies* 63 (S1): 38–54.

Lederach, John Paul. 1997. *Building Peace: Sustainable Reconciliation in Divided Societies*. Washington, DC: United States Institute of Peace.

Lowi, Theodore J. 1999. Frontyard Propaganda: A Response to "Beyond Backyard Environmentalism". Boston Review. October 1.

MacDonald, Rhona. 2005. How Women Were Affected by the Tsunami: A Perspective from Oxfam. *PLoS Med* 2 (6): e178.

MacKenzie, Michael K. and Mark E. Warren. 2012. Two Trust-Based Uses of Mini Publics in Democratic Systems. In *Deliberative Systems: Deliberative Democracy at the Large Scale*, ed. John Parkinson and Jane Mansbridge, pp. 95–124. Cambridge: Cambridge University Press.

Mansbridge, Jane. 2009. A "Selection Model" of Political Representation. *Journal of Political Philosophy* 17 (4): 369–398.

Mansbridge, Jane, James Bohman, Simone Chambers, David Estlund, Andreas Føllesdal, Archon Fung, Cristina Lafont, Bernard Manin, and José Luis Martí. 2010. The Place of Power and the Role of Self-Interest in Deliberative Democracy. *Journal of Political Philosophy* 18 (1): 64–100.

Mansbridge, Jane, James Bohman, Simone Chambers, Thomas Christiano, Archon Fung, John Parkinson, Dennis F. Thompson, and Mark E. Warren. 2012. A Systemic Approach to Deliberative Democracy. In *Deliberative Systems: Deliberative Democracy at the Large Scale*, ed. John Parkinson and Jane Mansbridge, pp. 1–26. Oxford: Oxford University Press.

Mendeloff, David. 2004. Truth-Seeking, Truth-Telling, and Post-Conflict Peacebuilding: Curb the Enthusiasm? *International Studies Review* 6 (3): 355–380.

Milewicz, Karolina and Robert Goodin. 2018. Deliberative Capacity Building through International Organizations: The Case of the Universal Periodic Review of Human Rights. British Journal of Political Science 48 (2): 513–533.

Mitchell, Ian, Anita Käppeli, and Hauke Hillebrandt. 2017. Commitment to Development Index 2017. Washington, DC: Center for Global Development. Available at: www.cgdev.org/publication/commitment-development-index-2017 accessed 3 June 2019.

Montanaro, Laura. 2018. *Who Elected Oxfam? A Democratic Defence of Self-Appointed Representatives.* Cambridge: Cambridge University Press.

Moser, Susanne C. and Lisa Dilling. 2011. Communicating Climate Change: Closing the Science-Action Gap. In *The Oxford Handbook of Climate Change and Society*, ed. John S. Dryzek, Richard B. Norgaard, and David Schlosberg, pp. 161–174. Oxford: Oxford University Press.

Muzaka, Valbona. 2010. Linkages, Contests and Overlaps in the Global Intellectual Property Rights Regime. *European Journal of International Relations* 17 (4): 755–776.

Narayan, Deepa, Raj Patel, Kai Schafft, Anne Rademacher, and Sarah Koch-Schulte. 2000. *Voices of the Poor: Can Anyone Hear Us?* New York: Oxford University Press.

NASA et al. 1986. Atmospheric Ozone, 1985. *World Meteorological Organization Global Ozone Research and Monitoring Project Report* 16. Geneva: World Meteorological Organization.

Neumayer, Eric and Thomas Plümper. 2007. The Gendered Nature of Natural Disasters: The Impact of Catastrophic Events on the Gender Gap in Life Expectancy, 1981–2002. *Annals of the American Association of Geographers* 97 (3): 551–566.

Norgaard, Richard B. 2008. Finding Hope in the Millennium Ecosystem Assessment. *Conservation Biology* 22 (4): 862–869.

Nye, Joseph S. 2001. Globalization's Democratic Deficit: How to Make International Institutions More Accountable. *Foreign Affairs* 80 (4): 2–6.

Odell, John. S. 2000. *Negotiating the World Economy.* Ithaca, NY: Cornell University Press.

O'Flynn, Ian. 2017. Pulling Together: Shared Intentions, Deliberative Democracy and Deeply Divided Societies. *British Journal of Political Science* 47 (1): 187–202.

Olson, Mancur. 1982. *The Rise and Decline of Nations*. New Haven, CT: Yale University Press.

Omelicheva, Mariya Y. 2009. Global Civil Society and Democratization of World Politics: A Bona Fide Relationship or Illusory Liaison? *International Studies Review* 11 (1): 109–132.

Oreskes, Naomi and Erik M. Conway. 2010. Defeating the Merchants of Doubt. *Nature* 465: 686–687.

Ostrom, Elinor. 2010. Polycentric Systems for Coping with Collective Action and Global Environmental Change. *Global Environmental Change* 20 (4): 550–557.

Panke, Diana. 2014. The UNGA—a Talking Shop? Exploring Rationales for the Repetition of Resolutions in Subsequent Negotiations. *Cambridge Review of International Affairs* 27 (3): 442–458.

Parkinson, John and Jane Mansbridge, eds. 2012. *Deliberative Systems: Deliberative Democracy at the Large Scale*. Cambridge: Cambridge University Press.

Parkinson, John and Declan Roche. 2004. Restorative Justice: Deliberative Democracy in Action? *Australian Journal of Political Science* 39 (3): 505–518,

Peltzer, Karl, Cheikh I. Niang, Adamson S. Muula, Kasonde Bowa, Linus Okeke, Hamadou Boiro, and Chiweni Chimbwete. 2007. Editorial Review: Male Circumcision, Gender and HIV Prevention in Sub-Saharan Africa: A (Social Science) Research Agenda. *Journal of Social Aspects of HIV/AIDS* 4 (7): 658–667.

Peters, Anne. 2009. The Merits of Global Constitutionalism. *Indiana Journal of Global Legal Studies* 16 (2): 397–411.

Pettit, Philip. 1997. *Republicanism: A Theory of Freedom and Government*. Oxford: Oxford University Press.

Rao, Vijayendra and Paromita Sanyal. 2010. Dignity through Discourse: Poverty and the Culture of Deliberation in Indian Village Democracies. *Annals of the American Academy of Political and Social Science* 629: 146–172.

Rask, Mikko, Richard Worthington, and Minna Lammi, eds. 2012. *Citizen Participation in Global Environmental Governance*. Abingdon: Earthscan.

Rathi, Akshat. 2015. This Simple Negotiation Tactic Brought 195 Countries to Consensus. *Quartz* https://qz.com/572623/this-simple-negotiation-tactic-brought-195-countries-to-consensus-in-the-paris-climate-talks/ accessed 27 August 2018.

Ratner, Steven R. and Robert E. Goodin. 2011. Democratizing International Law. *Global Policy* 2: 241–247.

Raustiala, Kal and David G. Victor. 2004. The Regime Complex for Plant Genetic Resources. *International Organization* 58 (2): 277–309.

Reinhard, Janine, Jan Biesenbender, and Katharina Holzinger. 2014. Do Arguments Matter? Argumentation and Negotiation Success at the 1997 Amsterdam Intergovernmental Conference. *European Political Science Review* 6 (2): 283–307.

Rhodes, R.A.W. 1997. *Understanding Governance: Policy Networks, Governance, Reflexivity and Accountability*. Buckingham: Open University Press.

Riddervold, Marianne. 2011. From Reason-Giving to Collective Action: Argument-Based Learning and European Integration. *Cooperation and Conflict* 46 (4): 563–580.

Risse, Thomas. 2000. Let's Argue! Communicative Action in World Politics. *International Organization* 54 (1): 1–39.

Sachs, Jeffrey. 2005. *The End of Poverty*. New York: Penguin.

Sass, Jensen and John S. Dryzek. 2014. Deliberative Cultures. *Political Theory* 42 (1): 3–25.

Schimmelfennig, Frank. 2001. The Community Trap: Liberal Norms, Rhetorical Action, and the Eastern Enlargement of the European Union. *International Organization* 55 (1): 47–80.

Scholte, Jan Aart. 2002. Civil Society and Democracy in Global Governance. *Global Governance* 8(3): 281–304.

Scholte, Jan Aart. 2016. Relations with Civil Society. In *The Oxford Handbook of International Organizations*, ed. Jacob Katz Cogan, Ian Hurd, and Ian Johnstone, pp. 712–29. Oxford: Oxford University Press.

Schrader, Christopher. 2018. Climate Talk: Tales of Hunger and of Hope. *Yale Climate Connections* https://www.yaleclimateconnections.org/2018/08/climate-talk-tales-of-hunger-and-of-hope/ accessed 22 August 2018.

Sen, Amartya K. 2003. Democracy and its Global Roots. *New Republic* 229 (14): 28–35.

Sen, Amartya K. 2009. *The Idea of Justice*. Cambridge, MA: Harvard University Press.

Sénit, Carole-Anne, Frank Biermann, and Agni Kalfagianni. 2017. The Representativeness of Global Deliberation: a Critical Assessment of Civil Society Consultations for Sustainable Development. *Global Policy* 8 (1): 62–72.

Shalom, Stephen. 2005. ParPolity: Political Vision for a Good Society. *ZNet* online: https://zcomm.org/znetarticle/parpolity-political-vision-for-a-good-society-by-stephen1-shalom/ accessed 3 June 2019.

Singer, Peter. 2009. *The Life You Can Save*. New York: Random House.

Singh, J.P. 2015. Global Institutions and Deliberations: Is the World Trade Organization More Participatory than UNESCO? In *Deliberation and Development: Rethinking the Role of Voice and Collective Action in Unequal Societies*, ed. Patrick Heller and Vijayendra Rao, pp. 192–222. Washington, DC: World Bank.

Smith, Graham. 2009. *Democratic Innovations: Designing Institutions for Citizen Participation*. Cambridge: Cambridge University Press.

Smith, William. 2018. Transnational and Global Deliberation. In *The Oxford Handbook of Deliberative Democracy*, ed. André Bächtiger, John S. Dryzek, Jane Mansbridge, and Mark E. Warren, pp. 856–868. Oxford: Oxford University Press.

Sommerer, Thomas and Jonas Tallberg. 2017. Transnational Access to International Organizations 1950–2010: A New Data Set. *International Studies Perspectives* 18 (3): 247–266.

Steffek, Jens. 2010. Public Accountability and the Public Sphere of International Governance. *Ethics and International Affairs* 24 (1): 45–67.

Steffek, Jens and Patrizia Nanz. 2008. Emergent Patterns of Civil Society Participation in Global and European Governance. In *Civil Society Participation in European and Global Governance*, ed. Jens Steffek, Claudia Kissling, and Patrizia Nanz, pp. 1–29. Basingstoke: Palgrave Macmillan.

Steiner, Jürg, Maria Clara Jaramillo, Rousiley C.M. Maia, and Simona Mameli. 2017. *Deliberation Across Deeply Divided Societies: Transformative Moments*. Cambridge: Cambridge University Press.

Stevenson, Hayley. 2013. Governing Climate Technologies: Is There Room for Democracy? *Environmental Values* 22 (5): 567–587.

Stevenson, Hayley. 2016. The Wisdom of the Many in Global Environmental Governance. *International Studies Quarterly* 60 (3): 400–412.

Stevenson, Hayley and John S. Dryzek. 2014. *Democratizing Global Climate Governance*. Cambridge: Cambridge University Press.

Stiglitz, Joseph. 2002. *Globalization and its Discontents*. New York: W.W. Norton.

Stirling, Andy. 2008. "Opening up" and "Closing Down": Power, Participation, and Pluralism in the Social Appraisal of Technology. *Science, Technology and Human Values* 33 (2): 262–294.

Stoker, Gerry. 2006. Public Value Management: A New Narrative for Networked Governance? *American Review of Public Administration* 36: 41–57.

Tallberg, Jonas, Thomas Sommerer, Theresa Squatrito, and Christer Jönsson. 2013. *The Opening Up of International Organizations*. Cambridge: Cambridge University Press.

UN. 2004. The Rule of Law and Transitional Justice in Conflict and Post-Conflict Societies: Report of the Secretary-General. Available at: www.un.org/ruleoflaw/files/2004%20report.pdf. accessed 3 June 2019.

UNFCCC 2014. Carbon Dioxide Capture and Storage in Geological Formations as CDM Project Activities. http://cdm.unfccc.int/about/ccs/index.html accessed 22 August 2018.

UNFCCC. 2015. Report of the Conference of the Parties on its Twenty-first Session. unfccc.int/resource/docs/2015/cop21/eng/10a01.pdf#page=2 accessed 26 October 2016.

UNFCCC. 2017. Fiji Momentum for Implementation. Decision 1/CP.23.

United Nations Development Group. 2013. *The Global Conversation Begins.* New York: United Nations.

von Einsiedel, Sebastian, David M. Malone, and Bruno Stagno Ugarte. 2015. The UN Security Council in an Age of Great Power Rivalry. United Nations University Working Paper Series, number 4.

Walker, Edward T. 2014. *Grassroots for Hire: Public Affairs Consultants in American Democracy.* Cambridge: Cambridge University Press.

Wampler, Brian and Janette Hartz-Karp. 2012. Participatory Budgeting: Diffusion and Outcomes across the World. *Journal of Public Deliberation* 8 (2): 1–6.

Wardak, Ali and John Braithwaite. 2013. Crime and War in Afghanistan: Part II: A Jeffersonian Alternative. *British Journal of Criminology* 53 (2): 197–214.

WCED. 1987. *Our Common Future: Report of the World Commission on Environment and Development.* Oxford: Oxford University Press.

WFUNA (World Federation of United Nations Associations) 2018. UN Security Council Presidency – Civil Society Dialogues. www.wfuna.org/sites/default/files/wysiwyg/docs/unsc_presidency_cso_dialogues_one_pager_2018.pdf accessed 14 July 2018.

WHO [World Health Organisation] and UNAIDS. 2007. WHO and UNAIDS Announce Recommendations from Expert Consultation on Male circumcision for HIV Prevention. 28 March. https://www.who.int/mediacentre/news/releases/2007/pr10/en/ accessed 12 July 2018.

WHO. 2002. Gender and Health in Disasters. www.who.int/gender/other_health/genderdisasters.pdf accessed 12 July 2018.

Young, Oran R. 1994. *International Governance: Protecting the Environment in a Stateless Society.* Ithaca, NY: Cornell University Press.

Zürn, Michael. 2018. *A Theory of Global Governance: Authority, Legitimacy, and Contestation.* Oxford: Oxford University Press.

# Acknowledgments

We acknowledge funding from the Australian Research Council, Laureate Fellowship FL140100154, 'Deliberative Worlds: Democracy, Justice, and a Changing Earth System.' Jonathan Kuyper acknowledges funding from the Riksbanken Jubileumsfond, project No. P-16-0242:1, 'Beyond Gridlock in Global Governance: Democracy, Politicization, and Legitimacy.' We thank Ana Tanasoca for work on an earlier draft, and John Braithwaite, Karolina Milewicz, and two anonymous referees for comments.

# About the Authors

**John S. Dryzek** is Australian Research Council Laureate Fellow and Centenary Professor in the Centre for Deliberative Democracy and Global Governance at the University of Canberra. Recent books include the co-edited *Oxford Handbook of Deliberative Democracy* (2018).

**Quinlan Bowman** is Lecturer in the Social Sciences Collegiate Division at the University of Chicago. He specializes in democratic theory and practice, history of political thought, philosophy of the human sciences, and pragmatism. Recent publications have appeared, for instance, in *Policy Studies* and *The Oxford Handbook of Deliberative Democracy*.

**Jonathan W. Kuyper** is a Lecturer in International Relations at Queen's University Belfast. His research focuses on the legitimacy of international organizations and negotiations. His work has appeared in the *American Political Science Review*, *European Journal of International Relations*, the *Annual Review of Environment and Resources* amongst other outlets. He recently edited a special issue on the legitimacy of global climate governance in *Environmental Politics*.

**Jonathan Pickering** is a Postdoctoral Fellow at the University of Canberra, Australia, based at the Centre for Deliberative Democracy and Global Governance. His research has been published in journals including *Climate Policy, Environmental Politics, Global Environmental Politics,* and *World Development*. He has co-authored with John Dryzek a book on *The Politics of the Anthropocene* (Oxford University Press, 2019).

**Jensen Sass** is a Postdoctoral Research Fellow at the Centre for Deliberative Democracy and Global Governance at the University of Canberra.

**Hayley Stevenson** is Associate Professor of International Relations at Torcuato Di Tella University, Buenos Aires. She is the author of *Global Environmental Politics: Problems, Policy and Practice* (Cambridge University Press, 2018), *Democratizing Global Climate Governance* (with John S. Dryzek, Cambridge University Press, 2014), and *Institutionalizing Unsustainability: The Paradox of Global Climate Governance* (University of California Press, 2013).

# Cambridge Elements ≡

# Earth System Governance

## Frank Biermann
*Utrecht University*

Frank Biermann is Research Professor of Global Sustainability Governance at the Copernicus Institute of Sustainable Development, Utrecht University, the Netherlands. He is the founding chair of the Earth System Governance Project, a global transdisciplinary research network launched in 2009, and Editor-in-Chief of the new peer-reviewed journal *Earth System Governance* (Elsevier). In April 2018, he won a European Research Council Advanced Grant for a research program on the steering effects of the Sustainable Development Goals.

## Aarti Gupta
*Wageningen University*

Aarti Gupta is Associate Professor of Global Environmental Governance at the Environmental Policy Group of Wageningen University, the Netherlands. She has been Lead Faculty in the Earth System Governance Project since 2014 and served as one of five coordinating lead authors of the recently issued ESG Science and Implementation Plan. As of November 2018, she is a member of the ESG Project's Scientific Steering Committee. She is also Associate Editor of the journal *Global Environmental Politics*.

## About the Series

Linked with the Earth System Governance Project, this exciting new series provides concise but authoritative studies of the governance of complex socio-ecological systems, written by world-leading scholars. Highly interdisciplinary in scope, the series addresses governance processes and institutions at all levels of decision-making, from local to global, within a planetary perspective that seeks to align current institutions and governance systems with the fundamental twenty-first-century challenges of global environmental change and earth system transformations.

Elements in this series present cutting-edge scientific research, while also seeking to contribute innovative transformative ideas toward better governance. A key aim of the series is to present policy-relevant research that is of interest to both academics and policy-makers working on earth system governance.

More information about the Earth System Governance project can be found at: www.earthsystemgovernance.org

# Cambridge Elements ≡

# Earth System Governance

## Elements in the Series

*Deliberative Global Governance*
John S. Dryzek et al.

A full series listing is available at: www.cambridge.org/EESG

Printed in the United States
By Bookmasters